PREEMIE PARENTS

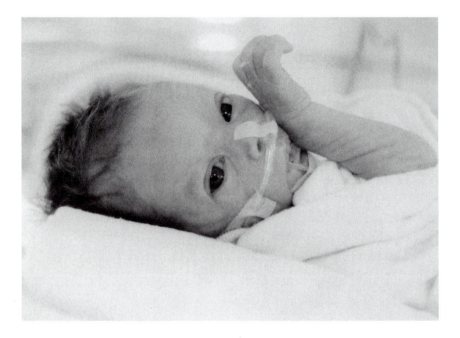

Preemie Parents

Recovering from Baby's Premature Birth

LISA MCDERMOTT-PEREZ

*With Eileen Penque, RN, Debra Ann Jones, MD,
and Juan Carlos Roig, MD*

Westport, Connecticut
London

Library of Congress Cataloging-in-Publication Data

McDermott-Perez, Lisa.
   Preemie parents : recovering from baby's premature birth / by Lisa
McDermott-Perez with Eileen Penque, Debra Ann Jones, and Juan Carlos Roig.
      p. cm.
   Includes bibliographical references.
   ISBN 0–275–98906–2 (alk. paper)
   1. Infants (Premature)   2. Parenthood.   I. Title.
   RJ250.M43   2007
   618.92'011—dc22   2006029525
British Library Cataloguing in Publication Data is available.

Library of Congress Catalog Card Number: 2006029525
ISBN-13   978–0–275–98906–4
ISBN-10   0–275–98906–2

First published in 2007

Praeger Publishers, 88 Post Road West, Westport, CT 06881
An imprint of Greenwood Publishing Group, Inc.
www.praeger.com

Printed in the United States of America

The paper used in this book complies with the
Permanent Paper Standard issued by the National
Information Standards Organization (Z39.48–1984).

10   9   8   7   6   5   4   3   2   1

Table of Contents

Foreword   *vii*
  by Amy E. Tracy

Acknowledgments   *ix*

Introduction   *xi*

1   Understanding and Preparing for a Preterm Birth   1

2   After Birth   13

3   The Unfinished Baby   25

4   Expecting the Unexpected   33

5   Jealousy   45

6   Going Home Alone   55

7   Baby Time and Bonding   63

8   Baby's Best Advocate   73

9   Views from Others in the Baby's Life   83

10 Self-Empowerment   99

11 Anxiety and Focus on the Future   107

12 Inspiration and Hope   119

13 What Happens to Dad   135

14 When All Else Fails   143

Appendix A Definitions of Common Terms Heard in the NICU   *149*
Appendix B Medications and Side Effects   *155*
Appendix C Resources and Support   *159*
Selected Bibliography   *163*
Index   *165*

Foreword

When Lisa McDermott-Perez's daughter was born prematurely, her experience as a mental health professional helped her cope, but even she admits it was the emotional rollercoaster ride of her life. Myriad feelings, including those of guilt (Did I do something to cause my baby's early delivery?), anxiety (Will my baby be okay?), and fear (What will my baby's future hold?) go hand-in-hand with parenting a critically ill baby, and all preemie parents need some guidance. By combining her personal experience with her professional knowledge, Ms. McDermott-Perez has created a much-needed guidebook to lead preemie parents through this emotional journey.

With the continuing increase in preterm births and advances in life-saving medicine, there has also been an increase in preemie-care books; few, however, are entirely dedicated to the psychological needs of families or written in such a way that the stressed mom and dad can quickly read and understand. *Preemie Parents* does both. In a compassionate, empathic voice that only can come from someone who has been there, the book answers such questions as: Why do I feel this way? Are my worries normal? Is it okay to feel jealous? Why is my family reacting this way? Equally important, Ms. McDermott-Perez provides practical ways for coping and for empowering moms and dads to be better parents.

Parents with babies in the NICU (and possibly other children at home) have little time for focusing on themselves. But to help your baby become healthy and strong, you need to be healthy and strong. Take the time to take care of yourself by reading this book. Remember: Your emotional health is vital to your baby's well-being.

This book should also be handed to mothers and fathers at the same time they are told their pregnancy is "at risk." It should be part of the educational material NICUs give to their families. And it should be read by any healthcare provider who is part of the caregiving team, providing them with invaluable insight into the emotional world of the preemie family.

By Amy E. Tracy, *Your Premature Baby and Child* (Berkley, 1999) and *The Pregnancy Bed Rest Book* (Berkley, 2001)

Acknowledgments

My boundless love and gratitude to my three angels, Krista, Nicole, and Alissa, who are my source of strength. To my husband, Will, my mother, Noreen, and Les, for their endless support.

A special place in my heart for my friend Alicia for staying by my side every step of the way, then and always. A special thank you to all of my friends and family who assisted and supported our efforts in putting this book together.

There have been so many wonderful people that made the birth of our daughter and so many other parents' difficult journeys just a little bit easier.

Dr. Seth Herbst, from the Institute for Women's Health and Body, for his friendship, support, and encouragement in the darkest time of our lives.

Dr. Jorge Sallent and nurse Nadine, for the constant support and safekeeping of our angel as she progressed to the beautiful child she is.

The staff at St. Mary's Hospital, NICU, the nurses, the practitioners, and the respiratory therapists who dedicate their lives to saving babies.

Introduction

The number of premature births in the United States has risen dramatically in recent years, with premature low birth now designated as the number one obstetrics problem in the United States—affecting some 12 percent of all births. Other developed countries, such as the United Kingdom, where 1 in every 10 babies is born premature, also struggle with this issue. Preterm birth is the leading cause of newborns who are at risk for serious health problems. In the midst of these births, where a mother's arms and cheers of joy are replaced by high-technology incubators and cautious hopes for healthy life, there are the parents—parents whose mental strength and health may understandably wane in the face of the challenges and fears that accompany a premature child.

There are many medical texts with very helpful information about premature infants, but there are few that address the emotional trauma that is experienced with the birth of a premature infant. Knowledge is your friend in the journey of parenting a premature infant. It is a very unpleasant and painful experience that affects all members of a family and the medical staff who provide care for the newest addition to your family. In order to heal from this experience and move forward, we must all recognize our emotions and take a proactive role in the healing process.

As a parent of a premature infant and a professional in the mental health field, I understand the guilt, anxiety, fear, and host of other emotions that come along with parenting a preemie. Unfortunately, medical technology has not advanced to the point where we can predict with 100 percent accuracy what will happen in a pregnancy or in the future of a child who is born prematurely. While we continue to make medical advances, so many babies are born to mothers that are unaware that they will be having a premature baby. There are also others who know well in advance that they are a candidate for premature birth. Whichever category you may fall into, the challenges of coping with the hospital stay, mourning for the loss of the pregnancy, going home alone, and many other factors can cause intense emotions that, if left to linger, will make it more troublesome to face future challenges, which there will be plenty of.

Since so many parents of premature infants and their families experience many of the same emotions as they go through the trauma of a preterm birth, the subject of the emotional trauma of the families seemed worth addressing. I watched my own family's turmoil as the baby and I stayed in the hospital for a total of four months. Dr. Debra Jones, Dr. J. C. Roig, and Eileen Penque, RN, watch the turmoil the families go through daily. One of the most difficult aspects of the experience for parents and professionals is not knowing and understanding the emotions, reasons for reactions to others, and the general state of mind. The wealth of medical knowledge you are able to obtain serves as no comfort in calming the mind of a preemie parent.

This book is about providing positive, hopeful, and self-motivating thoughts for parents to develop the special bond with your baby, face your fears, and accept the challenges you and your baby will have, even in the most unfavorable of situations. By combining my background as a licensed mental health counselor with the backgrounds of Dr. Debra Jones, Dr. J. C. Roig, and Eileen Penque, whose daily experiences with premature infants continue, we hope to provide both parents and medical professionals with insight into the emotional turmoil that faces parents of premature infants, before and after the birth.

This book is organized in a manner that addresses the feelings as a parent may experience them on the road to recovery. While the book may seem as if it is, at times, geared toward women, the suggestions and tips that we provide can be beneficial to both parents individually and as a tool to support each other. Also provided is insight from the perspectives of nurses, doctors, and other parents who have had preemies born to them. Every parent brings to the experience their own unique life experiences, and therefore how parents experience the emotions will always be different. Our hope is that as you experience the ups and downs of the neonatal intensive care unit (NICU), you can find comfort in knowing that you are not alone and that you will survive. This book will give you insight and perspective on some very confusing emotions that, at times, can be overwhelming—an experience we refer to as parenting a preemie.

As medical professionals read this book, it is our hope that they will gain a better understanding of the parents who face the challenges and fears that accompany a premature child. As health care practitioners, we see the raw emotions of the families of these babies every day, and by providing a better understanding of the underlying causes of the emotions, it is our hope that parents and health care providers will find common ground in helping the family in the process of recovery.

The information in this book is a supplement to information that your own medical professionals provide. The information is intended as a self-help construct and does not replace the potential need for professional intervention.

BABY ALISSA

My experience began in the summer of 2004. I was six months pregnant and was doing all the preparation a woman with a child due in the next three months would do. My husband and I were fixing up the nursery, looking through name books, making the rounds at the hospital to choose the perfect birthing room, registering for my shower, and waiting for the perfect child to arrive. I never had any reason to suspect that my birth experience would be anything but typical. I had two children preceding this pregnancy, and they were both full-term pregnancies without complications. This pregnancy also had been progressing, by all accounts, normally. I was 37 years old at the time.

All the tests to ensure that the baby was progressing as expected had been done, including an amniocentesis. Every result was negative, but I felt something was not right. Sometimes, you need to trust a maternal instinct, and I did. This baby's movement was different from what I had experienced with my other children. I requested a biophysical, a fancy word for a real good look through an ultrasound, and it was at that time that we realized that this was not going to be an ordinary pregnancy.

My world stopped, and the baby shower, nursery, and everything else associated with preparing for the birth came to a halt. The main focus now became whether my child was going to live, and if she did, what could be expected for her future. My immediate concerns were disabilities, brain damage, and overall quality of life. With all the medical technology that was available, the only guarantee the doctors could give me was that my baby was going to be premature. With that one guarantee I put every bit of energy I had into preparing for a premature birth. There was little information in my favorite pregnancy books, and my quest for knowledge about premature infants became an obsession. When the books were not enough, I consulted with medical staff, friends, and experts, who sometimes gave conflicting answers to crucial questions. I found a wealth of information in the books I discovered, but in my search for answers, there was nothing that could prepare me emotionally for the birth of my child and what lay ahead. Surprisingly, all the personal accounts of premature births that I read had one common denominator: the same realm of emotions.

My daughter had been born at 29 weeks, and I had been sitting by her bed for weeks with positive thoughts and prayer, partly because I wanted her to get better, but also because I was too afraid to face my own fears that she may not survive or be a normal child. Sometimes it takes a dose of reality to force you to deal with difficult situations. My dose of reality came unexpectedly, and I was completely overwhelmed by the emotions it evoked. It was on that day that the baby girl in the incubator across from my daughter's passed away. As I was told of her passing, I remembered the day before how I had wished I could hear my child cry as she was. The cry seemed so normal for an infant. My daughter never seemed to cry, and at that time I would have given anything for my child to cry to be fed, changed, or soothed. As I came into the NICU on that day, the mother of this beautiful baby girl was holding her child and saying good-bye one final time. As if saying good-bye every night as we leave without our children was not difficult enough, this time was forever. It was that day that I realized how grateful I was and how difficult it was for each and every family member to sit in the NICU day after day, with nothing to keep us company but our own thoughts and fears. We made it through the roller coaster of emotions, and my daughter, now age three, survived and is a feisty ball of fire who I feel blessed to have been given the opportunity to mother.

In looking back on my own experience, at the time I would have felt selfish thinking about my own mental health when my child was lying in an incubator needing assistance just to take a breath. What I took away from the experience as I watched my child improve—and as others were not so lucky—is that the state of mind of the parents has a significant impact on the well-being of the infant. Accepting that you have an infant who is premature and being able to master the skills of patience and calm when your "perfect baby" has been thrust into a world of high-tech medical machines will be as challenging as addressing your own emotions.

The experience can be so painful and such an emotional challenge for you and your family that it is our hope that by sharing our knowledge with those who are facing the challenges of parenting a premature infant, they will gain an understanding of their own emotions and be able to acknowledge their fears and accept the challenges. While we celebrate the successes, we have to acknowledge that the early delivery of a child brings monumental challenges for parents, health care professionals, and our community as a whole.

There are two ways to live your life.
One is as though nothing is a miracle.
The other is as if everything is.

—Albert Einstein (himself a preemie)

Chapter 1

Understanding and Preparing for a Preterm Birth

Every pregnancy is different, as is every child. Some women learn very early on that they are high risk and have the potential of having a premature infant; others only find out that the baby will be premature when they are in labor. No matter what the situation, there are few guarantees of the outcome. Each and every parent who is waiting for the unexpected wants a guarantee—something to hang your hat on, something that you can count on. One guarantee is that you are going to be in a hospital with a neonatal staff if you are delivering a premature infant; a second guarantee is that you will not have all of your questions answered immediately. The first day or two and how your child adjusts outside of the safety of the womb will be critical. As days go by and you meet the neonatal staff and monitor your baby's progress, your questions will begin to be answered. One of the first steps on this journey is learning patience.

MY BABY IS GOING TO BE PREMATURE

When you are told that you might deliver a premature infant, the fear that you experience engulfs every part of your body—the fear of the unknown. So many women go through their pregnancies without complications that most of us live in a bubble as to the risks of childbirth for the mother and the child. It seems inconceivable that when you are told you may have a premature infant, you are required to conquer all the anxiety and fear because it is in the best interest of the child. You can, and you will. Your maternal instinct to protect and nurture your children will always help you to overcome obstacles. One of the most significant things to remember is that your stress level is the baby's stress level; being able to ease your mind will relax your body. Many women classified as high-risk pregnancies may be ordered to bed rest in or out of the hospital. Not many of us can envision being confined to a bed with a family, a job, and so much to do to prepare for the baby. What you need to remember is that the doctors have promising medical reasons for ordering this prescription, and all the motivation you need is to know that you are protecting your baby's health.

Three of the best medical reasons for a woman to follow a doctor's orders follow.

- Your fetus is dependent on the blood that circulates from the placenta for its supply of nutrients and oxygen, and this blood flow is the greatest when a woman is resting.
- The time off your feet will boost blood flow to the baby, which will lead to a greater output of amniotic fluid, and this fluid is also less likely to leak out if you are lying down. This theory also has to do with gravity: Lying down puts less pressure on the cervix.
- Blood pressure has been shown to be higher in women who are walking about.

Bed rest can also be a stress reducer; the focus is on you and your needs, concerns, and symptoms. Your emphasis is shifted from doing your daily routines to simply concentrating on the baby and you.

There is a correlation between what a mother thinks and how the baby develops. Researchers believe that a mother who is experiencing extreme stress produces a significant number of stress hormones, called catecholamine, that affect emotions. If the baby feels enough stress, it can actually cause damage to the baby's nervous system. Some researchers believe that colicky babies are the result of a possible disturbed nervous system.

If you are ordered to bed rest, the baby will continually be evaluated during your pregnancy, including with a nonstress test (NST), which is used to determine if the baby is getting adequate oxygen. The baby's heart rate will also be evaluated and monitored. The baby will receive a biophysical profile, which combines the NST and ultrasound, to determine if the baby is getting adequate oxygen but also to check fetal breathing, fetal movement, and fetal tone and to determine the amount of amniotic fluid.

We hope to have persuaded you that you have no choice but to follow doctors' orders; even if you do not necessarily agree, the risk of being wrong is considerable. Although bed rest is meant to curtail stress, it also can be a source of stress. For those of you who are task or goal oriented, you have to consider staying in bed a job, a duty, or a chore, whichever fits your lifestyle. Each day that you are able to follow doctor's orders is an accomplishment. The following is a list of suggestions for those who have been ordered to bed rest.

- Set goals for yourself as you do with children; if you are good, then reward yourself with a massage or a treat. Just because you are bedridden does not mean you cannot indulge.
- Resting in bed day after day is going to give you the aches and pains. Try to do light exercises in your bed—with the consent of your doctor, of course. Your doctor may be willing to order a physical therapist if you are on complete bed rest. Some light exercises might include leg lifts, leg bends, head rolls, and shoulder shrugs. Popular stores stock the equivalent of oversized rubber bands, which are useful for stretching and resistance.
- Stay clean and attractive; this has a major impact on how you feel about yourself. Think about how fresh you feel after a warm, bubbly bath and a fresh coat of makeup or even a splash of perfume. Do not be embarrassed to ask your local hairdresser or manicurist to make house calls.
- Make your room attractive and functional; know morning from evening when the sun shines and when you can get a cool breeze. Open the windows and listen to the birds, or even to the traffic going by, to keep yourself connected to the outside world. Put up family photos or pictures of your favorite places to visit.
- Organize your space. Remember that you are in bed for the long run, so you will need more than a box of tissues and a bottle of water for the day. Decide what you will do on each day, whether it be a hobby or computer work. Ask your family to participate in helping you prepare for projects you have set for the day. If your family ends up being your gophers throughout the day, tension will increase.
- You should remember to keep your diet high in fiber and drink at least eight glasses of water a day. This will help to prevent constipation. Should you become constipated, consult your physician before taking any type of stool softener.

Remember that bed rest is just as tough on your family as it is on you. Your children do not understand the complexity of why you cannot meet their every need. You also may feel bitter as everyone else is able to move around the house. Remember that this is a family project and that everyone must make adjustments. The house can run without you; it may not run as effortlessly or in the same manner, but they will be able to manage.

As your life is changing, so are your emotions. Everything else has been turned upside down, and your emotions are no different. This is the beginning of the emotional roller coaster journey that comes with parenting a preemie. Some of the common emotions and their etiologies follow.

- Depression—Depression is probably one of the most common and lingering states that you will have throughout this journey. This is ok; you are normal. You have just completely changed your lifestyle and are preparing for the unknown. You feel a sense of abandonment for your everyday responsibilities.
- Irritability—What do they expect? Of course you are going to be irritable. You are basically chained to a bed every day or for the most part of every day, depending on the degree of bed rest that has been ordered. You do not know what you are going to do, day after day in a bed. This also is a normal emotion. Take the time to explain to your children or family that your irritability is not with them, but with the situation. I find that children learn best by example. If you have other children, have them stay in bed with you for as long as they can. Children have such energy that they usually do not last very long, but you will find a sense of enjoyment having the company, and it is hoped that they will understand how difficult staying in bed is.

One particularly insensitive sentiment that so many women were told by friends and family is that they wish *they* could stay in bed. For the first day or two it may seem great to relax, but anyone that has been bedridden for any length of time knows what a difficult feat it is. Remember that what you have to do is for your baby, and you want to think of it as a positive thing. The more you remark how "horrible" it is, the more difficult you make it on yourself to continue. Ninety percent of accomplishing this task is how you react to it.

- Anxiety/fear—Anxiety is created by your own thoughts. Try to keep your anxiety-provoking thoughts to a minimum. You cannot change what is about to happen to you or your baby. The best that you can do is to follow your doctor's orders. No matter what happens, you will know that you did all that you can do to keep your baby safe. Try keeping a calendar on the wall, not of how long you have been in bed, but of how many weeks you have been able to keep your baby safely inside the womb. Every week closer to your due date decreases the likelihood of complications with the baby.
- Boredom—Day after day of the same routine . . . we all need a little change. Switch things around in your day. Have breakfast for dinner. Watch a television program you never watched before. Other tasks might include studying something new, looking into your family's origins, listening to books on tape, or writing a journal for your baby about the experience.

Ask your health care provider about home uterine activity monitoring (HUAM). Although not considered to decrease the incidence of preterm delivery and considered experimental, HUAM can help a woman at home on bed rest. The comprehensive nursing program includes daily nursing visits that can evaluate the progress of the pregnancy. It also helps the patient not to feel so isolated and can alleviate many of the fears that accompany a high-risk pregnancy.

UNDERSTANDING WHAT TO EXPECT

The following is a general guide to help you to understand how your baby will be defined in the world of premature infants. You will find that many hospitals and doctors will refer to your child in kilograms, rather than in pounds. The following definitions of birth weight are the most recent rankings.

Normal birth weight infants	2,500 grams or more = 5.5 pounds or more
Low birth weight infants	1,500 to 2,499 grams = 3 pounds 5 ounces to 5.5 pounds
Very low birth weight infants	1,000 to 1,499 grams = 2 pounds 3 ounces to 3.5 ounces
Extremely low birth weight infants	less than 1,000 grams = less than 2 pounds 3 ounces
Micropreemies	less than 750 grams = less than 1 pound 11 ounces

It is during the last four weeks of pregnancy that your child will gain the most weight, so if your child is born prematurely, it will not be remarkable for him to fall into one of the above classes. Most premature infants lose this last four weeks in the womb, so they will not come out with the fat cheeks and thick, chunky legs you expect. The gestational age of the baby at birth will be a determining factor in your baby's birth weight. The earlier the birth, the smaller the baby. If your baby is born prior to 30 weeks, do not be shocked if your baby is very thin and looks somewhat underdeveloped. For all intents and purposes, your child will look undernourished. This statement is not meant to be shocking, but a significant part of processing your feelings during the trauma of the birth experience is confronting reality. There are numerous resources listed in this book that can provide specific information on what to expect for the gestational age at the time of birth.

This information plus the input of your pediatric physician will provide you with the most accurate information. If you are concerned that your baby will be born prematurely, I encourage you to research the information that is available—knowledge is power.

Some generalities relating to gestational age follow.

Less than 28 Weeks

Babies who are born less than 28 weeks have the most complications. Each child is different, and the circumstances and medical conditions have a direct impact. These babies are usually between one and two pounds and almost always require oxygen, surfactant, and machines to assist them in breathing. When a baby is this young, he has not developed the suck and swallow reflex and is usually fed intravenously until he is able to develop this function. Some cannot cry or are impeded by the mechanisms in their mouths. Because they were not ready to be brought into the world, they tend to sleep a lot. Their muscle tone is also not fully developed, so they may move very little. Keep in mind that children born at this age are going to look very different than a full-term baby. They may still be covered with a soft, lightly colored hair, called lanugo. You may also notice that their skin is very wrinkled and that they appear thin, with almost translucent skin. Although they may have an extended stay in the NICU, they have a chance for survival. Unfortunately, these children may continue to suffer from serious and long-lasting difficulties.

28–31 Weeks

If your baby is born between 28 and 31 weeks of gestation, he will look quite similar to a full-term newborn, but quite a bit thinner. The good news is that these children have a 90–95 percent survival rate. Many will initially require treatment with oxygen, surfactant, and medical technology. Their nervous systems at this gestational stage and earlier may not be fully developed and touching the baby may be limited. They will either have or will be beginning to develop the suck and swallow reflex and can be fed breast milk, either directly from the breast or from a feeding tube (placed down the nose and into the stomach). Keep in mind that your baby should still be in the womb. They tend to act as if they are still inside the womb, even when they are born. The baby may be able to grasp your finger but may only stay awake for short periods of time. The NICU will attempt to duplicate the womb by using artificial means such as incubators. Although this group is at risk for complications, they may not be as severe as those with an earlier gestational birth.

32–35 Weeks

If your baby is born at this gestational age, he has a 98 percent survival rate. Most of the babies born at this age have a birth weight of between three and seven pounds and appear just slightly thinner than a full-term baby. Most of these babies are able to breathe on their own, although some may need additional oxygen support or, depending on other medical conditions, may need additional medical technology. Babies born at this gestational age are unlikely to develop serious disabilities. However, parents should be aware that in the future, these children may experience learning and behavioral problems.

36+ Weeks

These babies are so close to being full term that they rarely require any special care after birth. They usually weigh between four and eight pounds and appear to be healthy, but slightly on the thin side. Some may experience minor problems, but these babies are usually short-term NICU patients and are unlikely to develop disabilities.

There are a lot of scary statistics out there about the survival and long-term health issues of premature infants. Keep in mind that everything you read is a statistic and does not relate directly to your child. Each child is different. We want you to have the information so that the shock factor is lessened, but we want you to keep in mind that the range of outcomes is wide.

A large part of preparing for a premature birth is alleviating the shock factor. You may want to visit your local NICU. Most of these units are off limits to visitors who do not have children in the unit, but your doctor can usually make arrangements for you to visit the unit prior to your baby's arrival.

The neonatal unit is divided into levels 1, 2, and 3. Level 1 facilities are for women who are having normal delivery and mostly full-term, healthy babies. Level 2 facilities will more than likely have a neonatologist on staff, and the nursery can usually handle more complicated births. Level 2 facilities usually handle up to 32-week babies. Level 3 is the most intensive treatment and is reserved for critical children who need constant care and monitoring. Each hospital is set up differently; when you visit your local hospital, do not be afraid to ask questions. This is your baby, and you want to know how your baby will be cared for and—of equal importance—how you can participate in the care. As we will discuss in future chapters, you have the ability to bond with your child in spite of the incubators and mechanical monsters of the NICU.

When you visit the NICU, keep in mind that despite the cold, sterile environment, this is only a temporary house for your child. The more comfortable you make yourself with this unit, the more comfortable your baby will be. Remember that inside or outside the womb, your baby responds to your reactions.

MOURNING THE LOSS OF THE PREGNANCY

Every woman that becomes pregnant has high expectations of what pregnancy will be like. It is expected to be a momentous, joyful experience for most women and their families. The first trimester is filled with the excitement of telling friends and family, choosing names, and the anticipation of a future with a perfect baby. Families develop pictures in their minds of what the baby will look like, sound like, or grow up to be. During the second trimester—when a woman feels the baby's movements for the first time, when the family is able to see the baby on an ultrasound, and when the sex of the child can be determined—families, and women especially, launch into the nesting mode, looking at baby clothing and beginning work on the nursery. The third trimester is when the true bonding occurs. It is at this time that your baby is waking and sleeping, kicking and punching, even hiccuping. What has been identified on a physician's screen as a baby is now real in mind and body.

When a woman brings a child into the world early, it is the end of a very special chapter in her life. When a child is born too soon, many mothers find it difficult to cope with the early termination of the pregnancy. There is little time to accept the loss of the pregnancy as their immediate need is to address the medical condition of the child. Unfortunately, for many women, children who are born too early are usually born in the third trimester. The delivery is quite different than what they were prepared for in birthing classes, and the tears of joy are usually mixed with those of fear.

During pregnancy, both parents experience prenatal attachment, and this attachment has significant effects on the infant as well as other maternal and familial outcomes. The mother's attachment to the child is much more physical than the father's since she is feeling the baby's movements more regularly than the father. Many women feel that they can sense the personality of the child even before birth.

The father experiences a similar prenatal attachment to the child but also experiences a sense of weakness in his powerlessness to protect his family when he cannot change the outcome.

When the pregnancy ends early, it is all too common for parents to have a strong grief response when the experience they expected is very different from the way they anticipated it would be. It is not only important to understand the grief and be able to work through it for the well-being of the child but also for the family. Families should be wary of letting their pain define them. Finding a venue to work through feelings of loss, which, unacknowledged, may become re-pressed and remain unresolved, is equally as important as caring for the child. A parent who is not emotionally healthy will have a more difficult time facing the challenges ahead.

The difference between women who have lost a child to death and those who have had a child prematurely is that there is no time to mourn the loss of the pregnancy. There is an immediate concern for the child and for what can be done to help the child. Many women feel that they may be selfish or that it is inappropriate to be concerned about what they wanted or wished for. What needs to be understood is that the child is special. The delivery was different than full-term deliveries, and as a family, you were not handed a perfect baby. If your child was born prematurely, then your path in life may be drasti-cally different than that of a woman who had a full-term baby. Fortu-nately, with medical technology today and specialists who understand the unique problems associated with premature infants, our children have better survival rates and more successes to celebrate.

GRIEVING YOUR PREGNANCY

Grief strikes us all at different times and in different patterns, but research shows that there are certain patterns associated with grieving, no matter what the loss. Grief is initially characterized by denial, numb-ness, agitation, and sobbing. In the case of a traumatic birth experience a person is not grieving a loss of someone but rather something that was very much a part of a mother's physical and emotional being. It is only natural to mourn the loss of the pregnancy. After the initial stages of grief, many women experience a rush of emotions for which they are unprepared. If you have been in bed for a long period of time, you may feel relief that the pregnancy has ended, and this can cause feelings of guilt. You may feel anger at God ("Why did you do this to me?") or the medical profession ("Why didn't you do something earlier?"). You may begin to doubt your faith in God or question the abilities of the professionals you are involved with.

To move forward from these feelings, it is necessary to seek ways of forgiveness and, at minimum, acceptance and understanding. Where the medical profession or your faith in God is involved, sometimes there are unrealistic expectations of what can be done.

PATTERNS OF GRIEF

Grief is an unusual emotion and is usually attributed to the death of a loved one. What many people fail to understand is that a person can grieve for many other things than a death. In this case you are grieving the loss of your pregnancy. This pregnancy was a part of you every day, and you developed an emotional bond to the child and the enjoyment you had from being pregnant. Do not be afraid to mourn this loss. Your baby was born too soon, and you missed many of the preconceived notions you had about the third trimester, your delivery, and bringing the baby home.

Grieving this loss may involve some long-lasting feelings that you did not expect. Not to mention, you are probably in the midst of worrying about your baby and what the future holds for him. Unfortunately, you need to address your own feelings to begin healing. There are certain patterns that grief follows, and by providing you with information about the progression grief takes, you will be able to recognize and move past these feelings with more comfort and ease.

Denial

Denial is usually the first response to a premature birth, whether you knew that you were going to deliver early or it was a sudden occurrence. Your body protects you from what is really happening when the experience does not seem real. You may feel a sense of numbness and not know where to turn. This is your mind blocking the reality. This stage is not only the initial stage of guilt, but also the initial stage of healing. It is a time to share your feelings and express your emotions. The birth of this child has impacted more than just one person. Sharing and expressing your emotions will not only be a healthy start for the healing process, but it will also bring you closer to your loved ones.

Anger

When things do not go as they should or as you have planned, you experience some type of anger. Your anger may be misguided, but it always exists. You may feel anger at the doctors who were not able to overcome the problems that caused you to go into preterm labor, or at your loved ones for not helping enough during the pregnancy, or at God because he caused this traumatic experience in your life. Start a journal, and list all the things that you are angry about. Be specific. You are entitled to this emotion, whether the anger is justified or not. This is a part of the process of grieving.

Guilt

Guilt is the anger that you have turned toward yourself. You will find yourself asking a list of never-ending questions, reviewing everything that you did or did not do that could have affected your pregnancy. While this is understandable, it is most likely that there is nothing that you could have done to prevent your baby from being born early.

Depression

The is the heavy heart that seems to be looming over every aspect of your life. In your mind, nothing will ever look the same or be all right again. Looking forward to tomorrow or anything else is an impossible and frightening thought. Depression can be isolating. You can strengthen your mental health by striving to keep your friends and family close; just knowing someone is there will have a calming effect. Your friends, family, and even the practitioners working with your child will help you with encouragement. Accept the encouragement, and know that your child needs you. A sense of belonging will also help you to increase your self-esteem and give you a feeling of purpose.

Acceptance

This is the final stage of grief, and as time goes by, you will begin to believe that you can make it through this experience. Accept what has happened, and find joy in the same things.

A family or woman experiencing grief may find that it manifests itself in physical symptoms as well as emotional. Physical symptoms can include extreme fatigue, pain, nausea, a tightness in your chest, headaches, loss of appetite, and difficulty sleeping. If physical symptoms continue, a physician should be consulted. Depression may need to be treated by a professional.

Some steps to follow in trying to keep both your physical and emotional strength follow.

- Keep a balanced diet, staying away from junk food, alcohol, and caffeine, which can dehydrate the body and give you headaches.
- Keep active—an active body is an active mind—even it is just a walk around the hospital or the parking lot. Activity and sunlight will also help to reduce your stress level.
- Keep a steady pace, and do not overload yourself. You do not have to do it alone. Try to maintain some semblance of a schedule.
- Keep enough time set aside for rest. Even when it is difficult to sleep, you should try to maintain a normal sleep schedule.
- Keep talking, and do not keep your emotions close to your heart. Talk about what you are feeling.

It is important to understand that you will mourn the loss of the pregnancy, but there also may be other areas of the roller coaster ride of parenting a premature baby where grief may apply. Try to take in the process of grieving and apply it to your circumstances. Throughout this book, you will find that every birth and NICU experience is different because we are all individuals who bring our own life experiences to the table.

Chapter 2

After Birth

Whether you had time to prepare for the early birth or were just thrown into the situation, you came to a point where you had to react. A psychological term for when a person experiences an immediate reaction to a stressor is sometimes referred to as the alarm phase of general adaptation syndrome. This syndrome, developed and studied by physician and endocrinologist Hans Seyle, consists of three phases: The first is commonly referred to as the alarm phase, also known as a "fight or flight" response, followed by the adaptation or resistance phase, and the third and final phase is referred to as the exhaustion phase.

If your child has been born, then you have already experienced part of the alarm phase. Your initial response was shock, and you were able to cope with the danger you saw. Either you were rushed to the hospital, or you were in a medical facility prepared for the birth. You faced the danger of giving birth to this child and pulled through. You were tense, you were nervous, but you controlled the crisis. The automatic response to fight kicked in, and you did what needed to be done to give your baby the best chance for survival.

General adaptation syndrome has associated with it not only an emotional response, but also a physical response. You and your spouse may have experienced dizziness, racing hearts, and perspiration in addition to disorganized thoughts. As the mother of the child, it would be hard to distinguish some of the physical symptoms from what generally would be expected during childbirth. However, one of the most important aspects of the response to the alarm phase for a mother to be aware of is that her initial response to the trauma decreases the effectiveness of her immune system, making her body susceptible to illness. You cannot care for your child if you are not physically and emotionally at your best. Most NICUs have strict policies about persons entering the NICU when they are ill because of how vulnerable the children are to germs, so be sure to do everything necessary to keep yourself in good physical condition.

As you recover from the initial shock of having your child prematurely and progress through the alarm phase, you may find that you have an onslaught of unanswered questions.

POSTTRAUMATIC STRESS DISORDER

Posttraumatic stress disorder deserves mention as the alarm phase of general adaptation syndrome has similar emotional and physical reactors. Posttraumatic stress disorder, commonly known as PTSD, follows the experience or witnessing of a life-threatening event. While most survivors who experience a trauma return to normal given time, others find that the stress associated with the trauma continues. In some cases it may even become worse. PTSD is recognized by people who relive the experience through nightmares and flashbacks. They may also have difficulty sleeping and feel detached or estranged to familiar situations. The symptoms can range from extreme to minor and may not necessarily be disabling.

While some of the symptomology may be consistent with what you experienced in your situation, you may find that the confines of the diagnosis of PTSD are limiting in that they do not address the continued traumas that you experience. PTSD also usually involves avoidance of the people, places, or things that bring the experience to mind. While it does happen, it is uncommon that as a parent, you will avoid the baby. The different types of anxieties, including PTSD, will be discussed further in chapter 11.

WHY DID THIS HAPPEN TO ME?

Why did this tragedy have to happen to my family? Was it something I did?

When most parents are preparing for the birth of their children, one of the last things they plan for is a premature birth. Most often, a couple has come to a period in their relationship where they are ready to develop their relationship into a deeper level of commitment and responsibility. During this time, couples' discussions of having children and starting a family begin to come to fruition. The planning stages include discussions of what you will and will not do as a parent: "I will never . . ."; "We won't . . ."; "I wish my mother had made me. . . ." As a couple, you may find yourselves discussing the color of the nursery, what you will name the child, or how long one of you will stay at home. As a mother, thoughts of gaining weight, nursing, Lamaze, and shopping are on the top of the list. During this planning stage it is highly unlikely that you will plan for a preterm birth. Who would know how? You have passed the first trimester, where every woman has in the back of her mind the possibility of miscarriage. You completed your second trimester of recognizing that your baby is a separate being and of bonding with that baby. You are just now starting your third trimester, and depending on how early your baby was born, you may not have had time to fear giving birth.

There are very few parents who realize the complications that can be associated with a pregnancy and preterm labor. If family planning included all of the risks and potential complications that could be associated with the birthing experience, I would confidently say that there would be far fewer births. As a doctor, there are two choices: enumerate all the problems that may possibly occur or cling to what is known and leave the unknown alone. Leaving the unknown behind spares the parents any stressful speculation and is the most common choice among physicians.

The question of why can be interpreted in two ways. On an emotional level, as a parent, you want to know why this burden has been placed on your shoulders. You are trying to make some sense out of something that makes no sense. You recognize that there is no definitive answer but find yourself asking anyway. From a physical standpoint you may want to know what went wrong. You will find both answers equally important in starting the process of healing from this life crisis. On an emotional level the question suggests denial and helplessness. Denial is an expected reaction in the adaptation phase to the birth of a premature infant. Working through the denial will be critical to you and your baby during the first days. If you are someone who is used to having control of situations, the sense of powerlessness and the denial together may subconsciously cause you to detach from your child—your mind's way of protecting you from the pain that could be experienced should your child not survive. Do not allow yourself to distance from your child because you subconsciously believe he may not survive. The thought is a fallacy that you should not accept easily. You were connected to this baby preconception. As you planned for his future, thoughts of nurturing, holding, and caring for this child, you developed a connection. Trying to deny this relationship to your child during the most critical stages of the baby's life will be detrimental to you and your family in the future, no matter the outcome.

You must confront your fears and the reality of the situation.

THE BAD MOTHER THEORY

I must be a bad mother if I cannot keep my child healthy and safe. I must not be cut out to be a mother. I do not know how to care for this baby. I do not know what to do or not do for this baby. How can I be a good mother to this baby when I cannot even touch him?

You look at your baby so frail and delicate in the NICU and feel like you just cannot do this. The feeling of not being able to move forward does not mean that you are a bad mother; it means that your afraid. You are afraid for your baby and for yourself and your family.

Women have been having babies for many years, and books are published year after year with new theories on how you should hold your baby, feed your baby, how the baby should sleep, how to soothe your baby—the list is endless. What you will notice is that over time, having and caring for a baby has changed. Some experts will say that research and studies have been conducted to determine what is best for your baby. Is there really anyone out that there that can say that any one way is 100 percent better than any other? Each of us survived the way our mothers cared for us, and no one baby is ever cared for identically to the next, in part because each baby has individual likes and dislikes, wants and desires. Your baby will not allow you to be a bad mother; your baby will express to you his desires and needs, even in the NICU. Follow your instincts, and physicians' orders, and you will feel instinctively what is right for your child.

COMMON CAUSES OF PREMATURE DELIVERY

While there are so many different factors that can affect a woman having a preterm birth, you can take comfort in the fact that you are not alone. In an average week in the United States, 9,596 babies are born prematurely; this represents 12.3 percent of all live births. Sometimes women go into preterm labor for no apparent reason. In some cases the doctors are able to catch the warning signs and prevent the baby's early entry into the world with the use of drugs or just good old-fashioned bed rest. Despite the numerous management methods used, the incidence of preterm birth has changed little over the last 10 years. There is much more uncertainty than certainty in the causes of prematurity. However, in some instances the causes can be identified. The most common cause of preterm labor is spontaneous preterm labor. This is when contractions begin prior to 37 weeks of gestation. The second most common reason is premature rupture of the membranes (PROM), commonly referred to as "breaking your water." This can lead to infection and many other obstetrical problems. This is a complication in approximately one-fourth to one-third of all preterm births. Other causes of preterm birth may include

- abnormalities in the uterus, which can interfere with a growing fetus
- an incompetent cervix, where the opening in the uterus is too weak and opens early
- bleeding behind the placenta
- diabetes, kidney disease, high blood pressure, toxemia
- if the baby is in fetal distress
- previous premature deliveries, second trimester abortions, or multiple abortions
- an age of younger than 12 or older than 40
- working long hours on the feet and under extreme stress
- smoking cigarettes or using drugs or alcohol
- carrying twins or triplets who press on the cervix
- having too much fluid in the sac
- physical trauma
- lack of prenatal care
- presence of fetal fibronectin in vaginal secretions after 22 weeks' gestation.

These are just a few of the more common contributing factors leading to an early delivery. What becomes apparently is that you do not always have control over your body or other aspects of your life. There may be one cause or a number of contributing causes to the birth of your baby, most of which you had little or no control over.

BARGAINING

Do not be ashamed—we have all done it. Most people find that they bargain at the lowest points in their lives, when they feel hopeless and see their lives spinning out of control. Bargaining is an attempt to find some miraculous solution through God, a higher power, or some other superstitious sign or omen: "I will be the perfect parent, if you let my baby get well"; "I will never ask for anything again if. . . ." When most people bargain, it carries a religious overtone, whether you were ever religious or not. Some people just look for signs, which can be another way of looking for the positives in the situation: "The baby needs less oxygen, so she must be doing better." Just as with denial, bargaining is a delay mechanism so that you do not have to face the reality of the situation.

Omnipotence is another defense mechanism when an individual dealing with emotional conflict or external stressors feels or acts if he possesses special powers or abilities and is superior to others. This is not a common reaction but worth mentioning should you recognize the signs. Most of those who have faith also believe that the doctors and other staff were given the ability to care for their babies and were placed in their babies' lives for a reason. Keep your faith but recognize the reality.

WHY DO I FEEL GUILTY?

Guilt is the most common emotion experienced among women who have had children born prematurely or with a disability. Before allowing yourself to descend into a stage of self-pity because of real or imagined mistakes, take into consideration the following: The person who will judge you most harshly is you. You cannot blame yourself for the early birth of your child. You cannot blame yourself for not carrying your infant to term. What happened to you happened to someone else somewhere before. You need to recognize that the feelings of guilt that you may be experiencing are normal but represent negative automatic thoughts. This pattern of limited thinking is called personalization. Personalization is the tendency to relate all the events that are happening around you to yourself. Think about why you are blaming yourself. Where is your guilt driven from? Be specific. Some of these questions may apply to you and help you to understand the feelings of guilt that are experienced by many women in similar situations.

Are You Focusing on One Detail of the Situation to the Exclusion of Everything Else?

You may be filtering the experience. Filtering is walking with blinders on—you are guided by this one detail and keep out all other aspects of the experience. Some of the things that will happen with your baby will be more alarming than others, but each plays an important role in your baby's overall well-being. You are unable to see everything that completes the picture. If you dissect your feelings, you may be passing over details that played an important role. Try shifting your focus and placing your attention on all the events that occurred. You have developed a mental theme in your mind, and you must find a way to change it.

Are You Thinking of Everything Concretely, in Black and White?

This pattern of thought can sometimes be called polarized thinking. Your interpretations of things are extreme. There is no level playing ground—it was either marvelous or horrific. In the world of medicine, nothing is black and white. Medicine is a science, an evolving process of trial and error. This pattern of extreme thoughts can lead you to believe that anything less than perfect is unacceptable. Look for the good, and magnify these events. Try thinking in percentages. Even if you find yourself partially to blame, putting the feelings into percentages can help you to direct your thoughts in a more positive direction.

Are You Jumping to a Conclusion Based on One Single Event?

You may be overgeneralizing—taking a single nugget of truth and making sweeping judgments based on that truth. Each baby is different, so do not jump to conclusions if things are handled differently by different medical providers. Some of the key words that may indicate overgeneralization are *never, always, everybody,* and *nobody.* This type of thought pattern can restrict you in your ability to make life-altering decisions for your baby. Try examining how much evidence you have to support a generalization. Keep in mind that there are no absolutes and that everything you think of must have a neutral term.

Are You Catastrophizing or Magnifying?

Do you find yourself with a lot of what ifs? You may find yourself always thinking the worst or emphasizing things out of proportion. You need to get things into proportion. Ask yourself, what are the odds? Try balancing the statements that you make.

These types of thought pattern will limit your abilities and may cause you to misinterpret what you see. Are you still blaming yourself for the premature birth of your child? If you have taken the time to analyze your thought patterns, you have probably come to the same conclusion that has been told to you over and over: This is not your fault. You could not have altered what happened based on what you knew at the time. Being able to recognize the signs that you may be internalizing the guilt without resolution is critical to healing. This is a difficult step to take and requires deep self-analyzation. If you are not ready to rid yourself of this negative self-talk, then try looking at this perceived failure as an opportunity to do better.

A certain amount of guilt in your life is necessary. As a parent, you will experience guilt for so many things you do or do not do while your children are maturing, and even continuing once they become adults. Every time you read an article or see something concerning parenting practices and child behavior, you will find some way to cast doubt on yourself. You will worry about how much you are doing or not doing for your children, and you will feel guilty about how much time you spend with them or do not spend with them. There is no formula for perfect parenting. Feeling guilt is a normal part of parenting, and a certain amount of guilt in parenting is healthy. How much guilt you feel, how realistic it is, and how you handle it are what is truly important. It is when guilt becomes persistent or becomes cumbersome in your own mind that you must concentrate on changing the behavior. When the self-criticism and intense feelings of inadequacy assume unhealthy levels, it can develop into depression.

Be able to recognize when these feelings are lingering too long, and be open to professional guidance when and if it becomes necessary. Some of the signs that your guilt may be turning into depression are

- feelings of emptiness and helplessness, with no sense of hope for the future
- physical problems, such as sleep disturbances, sluggishness, and various aches and pains
- loneliness that is initiated by keeping friends and family at a distance
- lack of trusting feelings, like no one is there with you
- extreme reactions to changes—the original trauma can trigger excessive distress over minor changes
- combativeness, which can be seen as quarrelsome or defensive or presented in angry outbursts
- excessive regret and self-talk such as "if only I did" or "I should have"
- addiction to drugs and alcohol in an attempt to numb the pain.

Fathers also may experience guilt over the early birth of a child. The guilt may be over actions they believe they could have or should have done to make things easier on the mother. Men usually will avoid guilt as a way of avoiding responsibility for their actions real or perceived. Your spouse may feel guilty over not helping enough or not paying attention to the pregnancy. Men will look almost anywhere for a reasonable explanation before they will look at themselves. This displaced anger often causes tension in the relationship. However, you have to expect that you and your partner will differ in your feelings and also in your way of coping. Each of you is an individual who brings different life experiences to the situation. When men do accept their guilt, they tend to punish themselves excessively. Keep the lines of communication open with your spouse. Share your fears, guilt, sadness, and any other emotions you may be experiencing. You both want what is best for your baby. Be supportive of each other, and maintain mutual respect. You will find that men are able to move past the guilt and can put the emotion behind them. Women tend to nurse the emotion and have a more difficult time with coming to terms before moving past the sentiment. If your spouse is able to move forward more rapidly than you, he will be a tremendous source of support for you in this emotional journey.

You have been presented with a child who is as special as you want him to be. Coming to terms with the changes in your life will be difficult, but the joy and unequivocal love you receive from that child will make everything worthwhile. Take charge of the energy and invest it into your life again.

THINK POSITIVELY!

Use your own experiences to fill in the blank.

> I am grateful for. . . . .
> my child's life. . . . .
> my family. . . . .
> my husband or significant other. . . . .
> the doctors and nurses. . . . .

I AM NOT ANGRY WITH YOU

If you find yourself saying this to others in your life, then you may be dealing with displaced anger. Many people unintentionally act out their emotions through anger. It is an impulsive action caused by feelings of resentment surrounding the circumstances of the trauma of birthing a preterm infant. Anger provides an internal energy that is sometimes much needed. However, displaced anger is usually harmful to you and, more importantly, can lead to hostility. Hostile people feel hopeless. Do not be afraid to feel anger; we were given the emotion of anger to help us solve problems.

By knowing that anger is coming your way, you can recognize it, take control of it, and direct it toward actions that will improve the situation. Be able to keep your eye on your goals instead of blindly punishing others around you. For example, if you are blaming your spouse for not giving you enough rest time, identify if this really is the problem that is causing your anger. If it is, then be open to the opportunity of resting now. You can develop a plan to solve or alleviate the problem and use the energy that the anger has given you to solve it.

If you discover that the anger you feel really has nothing to do with who or what you are expressing your anger to, then your anger is an attempt to minimize your anxiety, to protect your ego, and to maintain a defense mechanism. You are avoiding your real fears by refusing to face what is happening to you. You are simply shifting your emotion from one object or idea to another. It is time to face your real fears. You should identify what the real fears are—try writing them down, all of them. Each and every fear affects your life and the life of your child. Some fears may be as simple as "I am afraid of hospitals" or others as complex as "I am afraid of losing my child."

Second, try to identify how you handle each fear. The situation you are in is demanding and, to some extent, intimidating because it is new to you and your family. How do you respond to an intimidating situation? Do you respond with anger? Do you sit quietly? Do you do what you are told? Or do you become an active participant in whatever is going on? The situation may be the same, but do you more often than not react the same? How you manage the fear will determine how you overcome the situation.

Now we come to the first step in addressing your fears. You have listed the fears and are able to identify them in words. The first step to overcoming them is relaxing your body. Find a phrase that is appropriate for you that can be used as a cue to remind you to relax, for example, "I can handle this." When you feel your body tensing and fear creeping in, say the phrase and take a deep breath, close your eyes or tense your muscles, and release each muscle slowly while repeating your phrase. You may find that your anxiety level is too great at times. If you need to retreat from the situation temporarily, then do that. Take a walk, or get a breath of fresh air. Each of us has a different way of relaxing our bodies—find yours.

Once your body is relaxed, your must have an action plan. In order to develop an action plan, your goals need to be realistic. There are some things you have no control over. Write down how to address the problem and what will help you to overcome these fears. Unfortunately, when you are dealing with a premature infant, most of your fears are catastrophic thoughts. These type of thoughts typically cause the most anxiety. The only way to address these thoughts is to develop balancing thoughts in your action plan.

You have had the baby, and probably your greatest fear was that the baby would not survive. Well, your baby survived. Now your fears change: What will the baby be like? What will be wrong with the baby? What will our future be like? Medical technology has come a long way; balance your negative thoughts with positive thoughts. Your baby was born early and survived. In order to deal with some of the more catastrophic thoughts, you need to put them into perspective. Take all of your what ifs and find the positive side to them. List them down, the negative on one side of the page and the positive on the other. Experience the emotions associated with each column. Let your anxiety build over the worst case scenarios, and think about what your reaction would be. Is it as bad as you imagine? What is the most likely thing to happen if you are exposed to this fear? What could you realistically expect? Could others help you if the fear you have were to occur? You may not find all the thoughts comforting, but you are exposing yourself and, to some extent, taking away the initial shock of having these fears come to fruition.

Being prepared is such an important component in parenting a premature infant. We have the misfortune of having so many new emotions, decisions, and experiences that our thoughts can be discombobulated in a matter of minutes. You will never know what lies ahead as medicine is a science, and even the best specialists do not know all the answers. However, teaching yourself ways to deal with your thoughts and fears is a step in the right direction.

Chapter 3

The Unfinished Baby

As you begin the second stage of general adaptation syndrome—the adaptation, or resistance, stage—your body will physically adapt to the stressors it is exposed to, but your body will also provoke physical responses for what it may be lacking. For example, if you are not eating, you may experience a reduced desire for physical activity as your body is attempting to conserve energy. How you approach this stage physically and emotionally will determine whether you enter the exhaustion stage.

You are still in the adaptation phase of general adaptation syndrome, and you are trying to come to terms with what has happened. The unexpected reality of the delivery itself can sometimes be the hardest to overcome. You must now muster all the strength that you have to move on to the next step in this journey—accepting that your baby is different. You have delivered a preterm infant who was not finished preparing for the world outside the womb. It is now up to you, the medical staff, and medical technology to help this baby on his journey of recovery. NICUs report survival rates in the range of 80–90 percent, a very strong number and something to keep in the back of your mind as you struggle with your baby's medical issues. Babies who would have surely died 10 years ago are now given a 50-50 survival rate.

It may seem as if the world you dreamed of as a new parent has all but disappeared. You went through a terrible ordeal in bringing this baby into the world. Now you are going to be buying all new guidebooks, learning a new medical language, and meeting a whole new group of people that you never knew existed. Throughout this journey you will find patches of roses and things that are wonderful about the world you are about to enter. In the end you will know that this is what was meant for your life and the life of your child. The pain will never disappear, but if you spend your life mourning what you lost by not carrying your pregnancy to term or by receiving a less than perfect baby, you will not have the opportunity to enjoy all the patches of roses along the way.

ACCEPTANCE

The harsh reality of the situation you are in is that your child is not the same as a full-term baby. You are going to be by your baby's side in the NICU, where you will have to make some major adjustments to every aspect of your life. A good guide to follow is to assume that at minimum your baby will be in the NICU until at least the date you were due. This is almost a guarantee.

As a parent, you may be wondering why you cannot accept that your baby is different. Émile Durkheim, a French pioneer sociologist, coined the phrase *anomie.* Anomie is a state of mind where what is standard and acceptable by societal terms is in conflict with what is present. In other words, you, your family, and your friends all had a mental image of how your pregnancy would end. You would have the perfect baby, flowers, gifts, and a homecoming. Instead, you are experiencing what no one would imagine, an emergency delivery with a team of infant trauma specialists, a less than perfect baby, and most probably one that will not be going home within days of birth. What you have just experienced is a situation where societal norms are just not present. According to Durkheim's theory, "to pursue a goal which is by definition unattainable is to condemn oneself to a perpetual state of unhappiness" (www.durkheim.itgo.com/anomie. html). To continue to desire for something that cannot and will not exist will only make your family's happiness that much less attainable. You must find a way to move forward on this journey.

Some suggestions for moving forward and accepting what has happened may seem simplistic but may also help in forming a bond with your baby. Give your baby a name as soon as possible, and use the baby's name often. Remember that this baby is yours; touch your baby whenever possible. Preemies can sometimes be overstimulated by touch, so be sure to talk to the medical staff about how much stimulation your baby can have. Take pictures as you would with any newborn child. You will come to treasure those pictures as you recognize the accomplishments in the future. The pictures are also a great way to measure progress and growth, even on a short-term basis. Babies have a very rapid rate of growth, and great strides can be recognized in short time periods.

"I AM AFRAID TO SEE MY BABY"

You find it difficult to see your baby in the NICU with the all the equipment and the cold and impersonal atmosphere that exists. There may even be days where you just do not feel like going to the hospital at all. When a baby is born prematurely, it is not uncommon for a mother to feel some sense of detachment from the child. You are still overcoming the shock of the experience, and some of your feelings may be attributed to hormones. A woman's body produces a great deal of estrogen during the last five weeks of pregnancy. The body's inability to complete this cycle could cause some mothers to initially feel detached from the baby.

It may also be difficult for you to look at this strange-looking, tiny baby. He does not match all the images you had set forth in your mind of what your baby would look like. Be prepared for what you are going to see in your child. You may find yourself experiencing similar reactions to those in the alarm stage if you are not prepared for what you are going to see. The gestation time and other medical conditions will determine what your baby will look like. There are resources in this book on what to expect at the different stages of gestation.

Try to look at your extended stay in the NICU as a growth-producing experience. You probably saw your baby when he was born, briefly, so you at least have some idea what the baby looks like. Remember that the atmosphere the baby is presented in may be more overwhelming to you than your baby's appearance. When your baby left the delivery room, he was free of all the mechanical monsters that exist in the NICU. If you did not get an opportunity to see your baby after the delivery, ask your medical practitioners to tell you about your baby before you see him.

Your baby will now look much different attached to monitors and wires and some very foreign-looking equipment. Try to look past the unfamiliar sounds and monstrous-looking equipment to see what is inside that incubator: Your baby, not what you dreamed of or maybe had nightmares about when you found out the baby would be premature, but the real thing. Take in the reality of what you see. A baby that was produced by you. A baby with fingers and toes and eyes to look into. The memory of seeing this baby for the first time will be forever embedded in your mind. Try to make it a positive experience. The NICU will be full of policies and procedures that seem to limit you from seeing your baby, but keep in the forefront of your mind that they are there for the best interest of your baby and not to restrict your freedom or bonding with your child.

As always, with psychological symptoms come physical symptoms. Walking into the NICU brings out emotions even in the strongest of souls. The staff of the NICU expect that you will feel overwhelmed. Recognize some of the physical signs, which can be weak knees, dizziness, sweating, and a pounding heart, among others. This is not the time to try to maintain and keep your composure. Give yourself permission to cry. The feeling of being overwhelmed is common, so let your feelings flow. So many women feel that they cannot let go of their emotions because they are afraid they will not be able to regain their composure. As natural as the tears, you will regain your strength through releasing your emotions.

ANTICIPATORY GRIEF

You have seen your baby in the NICU, and you feel as if you are having trouble moving forward. The feelings you have for your child are undeniable, but with all the beeps and wires you have difficulty processing in your mind how the medical outcomes can be good. What you may be experiencing is something referred to as "anticipatory grief." While anticipatory grief is usually attributed to adults who are facing a terminally ill family member, it can also occur in situations where the outcome is unpredictable, such as in the case of a preterm infant. The experience itself is such an anomie that you really are not sure what to expect. Unfortunately, our minds tend to wander to the negative in cases of preterm birth. Anticipatory grief can be defined as feeling the effects of loss and grief before death even occurs. Most often, the cause as it relates to premature birth is fear: fear related to losing the baby, fear of losing your present family structure, fear of starting over, and fear of the unknown. Catch yourself from falling down this path. You may notice signs similar to those felt when mourning the pregnancy: Guilt, tearfulness, constant changes in emotion, anger, depression, denial, and fatigue are all symptoms of anticipatory grief. Some parents refuse to name their children for fear of becoming attached. It is a fallacy to think that if you have not named your child, the loss you may sustain will be easier. There is evidence to support that the opposite holds true: Parents that fail to name their children have a more arduous time with the grieving process.

Following the path to grieving the loss of your child is dangerous for a number of reasons: you will have a more difficult time bonding to your child for fear of losing him; you will not plan for the future—every step of parenting a preemie is being prepared for what might come; and most importantly, you will isolate yourself since most others will not share your thoughts. The doctors, nurses, and other members of the NICU team are there to save lives. Imagine what the NICU would be like if they felt they could not make a valiant effort to save each one of those precious lives.

"I AM ANGRY WITH THE DOCTOR"

With the exception of your spouse, the doctor is the closest person to you during this grueling time. The doctor is also the most logical place to vent your anger and frustration. Before your baby was born, medical technology gave you the ability to look inside the womb and see all of the baby's features in four dimensions. Fetal monitors can determine your baby's heart rate and what stresses the baby, test upon test can be done to confirm what chromosomal or medical abnormalities a baby may have, but medical technology cannot figure out how to keep the baby inside the womb safe and secure. Naturally, this is the doctor's fault, or at least his profession's, and you will blame him. However, blaming is the most self-destructive and damaging of the expressions of anger. You may feel anger toward the doctor that he did not catch the problem in time or that he is not doing everything possible to provide your baby with the best possible care. Blaming people may make you feel better, but all you are doing is projecting, literally or in your mind, "I am not going to let you get away with it." The problem with that statement is that the blame does not provide you with any changes. By blaming others you are not changing the situation; you still feel as helpless as you did before you placed blame. Do not give up the power to change the situation by wasting energy on blaming. It might actually be counterproductive for you. If the doctor has to justify his actions and feels criticized, he may pull back or become more cautious in the care of your newborn. While you want the doctors to be cautious, you have to remember that there are a number of new drugs and techniques that come out on the market daily. You want to have an open door of communication to ensure that everything possible is being done for your baby. Let us be realistic: With modern health care costs and the costs of malpractice insurance, doctors pay attention to parents' reactions. Your baby will always receive the best possible care from any doctor. However, shutting down the lines of communication with your doctor by expressing anger is only going to add to your frustration in the future.

As you talk to the medical staff, be conscious of what you are asking from them. As a parent, you will always have the feeling that you could be doing something better, changing a diaper, massage, and so on. Your own rejection and anger may cause you as a parent to complain often. We identify this as a help-rejecting complainer. This is a person who deals with her own emotional conflict by making requests to the medical staff to disguise her own feelings or hostility toward others. These feelings become apparent when the complaints are met with offers of assistance or advice, which is then rejected. Complaining, just like blaming, serves no purpose.

While we want you to be active in the care of your child, examine your complaints and make sure that what you are complaining about is not a projection of your own feelings.

GETTING ACCUSTOMED TO THE NICU

Now that your baby is here, it would seem reasonable to assume that if medical professionals could define so many different aspects of your baby's health inside the womb, they certainly should be able ascertain more now that the baby has arrived. This is true: A neonatologist will review all the work that has been done by your obstetrician and will also provide a hands-on assessment of your baby. This is the best possible place for your child, and your rational side will acknowledge this. Yet you may feel unwanted, and even unneeded, as all the professionals do their job in caring for your baby.

This will be your home away from home for an extended period of time. There may actually come a time when you feel sadness leaving the NICU. As difficult as it may seem to you now, treat the NICU as your home. The policies and procedures that are in place in the NICU may seem harsh, but they are intended to protect your baby. Each NICU facility is different, but ask what your baby is allowed to have. Depending on the condition of the baby, you may be able to dress your baby and place personal items in the baby's incubator. (Most babies that are in level 3 units are allowed to have little other than the medical necessities because the risk of contamination and germs is too extreme.) The first priority in getting comfortable in your new home is going to be establishing a routine. You are going to have to find a way to balance all your other home and life activities so that you can spend as much time with your baby as possible. We will discuss this at greater length in chapter 7.

Preemies who have been brought into the world too early share some common traits regarding medical needs. As you enter the NICU during the first weeks, it will be helpful for you to know some of the most common medical difficulties preemies face.

- Since preemies have very little body fat, they have difficulty staying warm.
- Many of these tiny miracles also have breathing problems because their lungs are immature and not fully developed.
- Preterm babies also have difficulty being fed as their digestive tracts are not completely developed, and they may not have developed the suck and swallow response.

These are very vague, generalized statements as they relate to premature infants. You should consult additional resources and your own medical providers for further information more specific to your child. As the days go by, you will learn more about your baby and his health concerns. A good suggestion for keeping track of everything that is happening with your child is to keep a journal. So many women describe the first few days as feeling as if they are in a fog. Keeping a journal will help if the information seems overwhelming to you. As time passes, you will find your journal to be a source of comfort as you watch your baby progress.

Later on, we will discuss how you can be a parent to your baby in the NICU, while helping to improve the overall quality of care that your baby receives.

REMEMBER YOU

Let us not forget that you are also a patient. If you have just given birth, whether you have gone home or are still in the hospital, you are still recovering. For those women who were in bed for any substantial period of time, the loss of muscle tone, lack of cardiovascular exercise, or an otherwise inactive lifestyle will contribute not only to your physical well-being but also to your mental well-being as well. Some of the physical symptoms may include dizziness and fatigue. You will not recover overnight and will require time to heal. If your premature birth was brought on by hypertension, eclampsia, diabetes, or any other medical condition that can continue past the pregnancy, your top priority should be taking care of you. You cannot care for your baby if you are not physically and mentally in shape.

ACCEPTING THE UNKNOWN

The time when your baby's hospitalization begins in the NICU is a slow process of adaptation, and although the chances for survival are great, you will experience many highs and lows throughout the term of your stay. Waiting will be the most difficult of tasks for you as a parent. Not knowing what to expect in the next few days or years will be troubling.

During the first few weeks your baby is in the NICU, it is not uncommon to find that you and your partner may be detached or appear cool about the situation your child is in. You are not calling everyone you know to announce the birth as expected, and you may not even desire visits from close friends or relatives. This is not uncommon—you are still recovering from the shock and are not sure what the future holds. Even if you do make the phone calls, you are not sure what to say. Try not to worry about your friends and family now. The frustration, fear, and shock over the experience can be projected in a negative way. It is better to express your need to be with your child independently than to have to apologize for your behavior later. You will have plenty of time later to explain your need to be alone with your child. Do not be alarmed if the reason you do not want visitors is because you do not want people to see your baby—a baby different than any baby magazine ever portrayed. It is not uncommon to feel as if you do not want to show off your baby with all the wires and machines attached. You can admit to yourself that you are having difficulty looking past all the medical monsters, and rather than subject yourself to feelings of concern as to what other people see, take time for yourself. Your friends and family will support you and be there when you and the baby are ready to meet the world.

Unfortunately, there is no crystal ball, and medical science has not come far enough to give the guarantees that you so desperately want to hear about your baby's health and future. The only thing that you can do is to master the skills of patience and calm. There will come a time when you have come to terms with the unknown and are willing to accept whatever challenges lie ahead.

Chapter 4

Expecting the Unexpected

Welcome to the world of what ifs and waiting. It is guaranteed that for the next two years, and maybe even longer, you will find yourself asking what ifs, and you will be waiting to see if the what ifs ever happen. The world of premature infants is a what if in itself. What if the baby is 30 weeks? What if the baby has a birth defect? What if my family does not understand? What if . . . ?

The real challenge is the waiting. If your child has been identified as likely to have birth defects or a disability, you will find that many of the doctors are not even able to tell the extent of the disability until your child has reached the age of two or older. Two years old, however, seems to be the magic number in many areas of development with regard to a premature infant. The statistics and probability of disabilities in your child will, in part, be determined by his gestational age and also by his medical status. This is the beginning of the ups and downs of parenting a preemie.

The NICU roller coaster is what most seasoned veterans of the NICU refer to as the emotional journey. After your feelings of distress and alarm at having a premature infant begin to fade, you are faced with the medical uncertainties that are commonplace in the NICU. When it comes to a preemie's health care, you will find that just as with your emotions, there is a pattern to the ups and downs. You will have reasons to celebrate and reasons to cry. There will be plenty of progress and an equal number of setbacks. The cornerstone of surviving the setbacks is to give yourself permission to experience the emotions. If you feel you need to cry, then do so; if you feel you want to celebrate, then do so. Yes, you are allowed to scream.

The waiting, on the other hand, will cause you to be impatient and, at times, feel helpless. A good example would be when the doctors make their rounds. It is commonplace in NICU facilities to have a specific time when no one from the outside is allowed into the unit. This is the time that the doctors, nurses, and other medical providers spend time consulting about your child. This is the time that you would most like to be present, when every provider is together discussing treatment plans and other important medical issues regarding your child. However, you usually will not be allowed. You will be forced to wait. You will wait to hear results of medical exams, you will wait to hear about consultations, you will wait to see if treatments work, you will wait for doctors to arrive—the list is endless. The control you have over the waiting is nonexistent.

While you cannot control how long you have to wait, the feelings of frustration, fear, and helplessness are real, and you do have control over them. Refocusing your attention to the present and not dwelling on what the future might bring will help you to relax and enjoy the miracle that has been brought into your life.

The feeling of frustration is part of the fear that you have of the unknown. You feel frustrated that you or the medical staff cannot "fix" your baby. You have the greatest of hopes for your baby but are also frustrated and feeling helpless that you cannot make your hopes and dreams come to fruition. In order to move forward and look to the future with positive hopes and dreams for your child, you must identify the realities of the situation versus the irrational fears that may be overwhelming your mind.

There will be time for hope and time for fear. You must learn to place hope first, even when your fears seem to overcome all the positive energy you have spent time cultivating.

REALITY RULES

It is essential that you make a concerted effort to overcome those fears that are irrational. Reality must rule in order for you to make rational decisions regarding the care of your baby. Irrational fears are beliefs that an event, which is happening, or the feeling that something is going to happen, will result in a negative, disastrous, or life-threatening outcome. The result of these fears is that they ending up ruling you. This could be dangerous for you as a parent as your underlying motive in the decisions that you make about your child will be related to the irrational fear. Irrational fears block your recollection, problem-solving, and decision-making abilities. You are writing a negative script with disabling beliefs that will prevent you from providing a healthy, positive outlook of what is to come for your child, now and in the future.

As a result of these fears, you may become resistant or hesitant, or even just completely unwilling, to participate in the nurturing and healing process. This is a negative belief system that will need to be replaced with positive affirmations and a mixture of a few doses of reality. The goal in identifying your irrational fears is to turn off these obsessing thoughts and identify a plan based on your rational fears and realistic outcomes.

The first step in overcoming your fears is to identify which fears are real and which fears are imagined. Start by listing all the fears that currently exist in your life. Try answering the following questions.

How real are these fears for me?
How much power do these fears play in my life?
How do these fears disable me?
What emotions do these fears block?
Are these fears influencing my decision making?
How do my fears affect my response to help from others?
What is the worst thing that could happen to me if I do not hold on to this fear?
What positive things might happen to me if I do not hold on to this fear?
What new behavior can I develop to confront my fear?
If the fear is real, is there anything I can do to change the outcome?

For example, if you fear that your child will be mildly retarded, you have identified this as a real fear. Now analyze the fear. How powerful has this fear been? Is it holding you back? Has there been any medical evidence to indicate that your child will be mentally retarded? Is this fear affecting the decisions you make or the help that you get from others? Let us assume that there is no medical evidence to back up this fear but that you read in a book that for your baby's gestational age, there is a 30 percent chance of mild mental retardation. Your next step would be to make an honest assessment of this fear and create a plan to overcome it. You have determined that this is a possibility that may be determined in the future. Is there anything that you can do about it now? What will happen if you set aside this fear? Once you have put this fear into a realistic perspective, it should no longer be a focal point of your energy and efforts.

1. You identified the fear.
2. You analyzed the fear.

3. You assessed the fear and developed a plan to overcome it.
4. You can now turn your focus to a more immediate need, preferably something that you can control.

By taking each fear and examining it thoroughly, you have taken the necessary steps to address the important here-and-now needs of your child. You are a parent now; there will be plenty of time for worrying in the future.

EXPLORE YOUR OPTIONS FOR SUPPORT

Although no two experiences can be identical, you will find that families of premature infants share similar experiences. In an attempt to protect patient privacy, the medical staff cannot direct you to children with similar concerns or parents who are currently patients, but they may direct you to NICU graduates who wish to share their experiences. While patient confidentiality is important and respect for privacy is essential, connections that you make in the NICU can be shared for a lifetime. In an age of computer blogs, chat rooms, and other online sources where we can share our deepest emotions with total strangers, we sometimes neglect what is right before us: The importance of connecting with other NICU families. Each of you is at a similar stage in the recovery experience from having a traumatic birth, and sharing the emotions, triumphs, and setbacks with other families as you manage your life in the NICU, you may learn and share tips that can help both of you in your journey. As you share your experiences, you want to be careful not to compare your babies. Each baby has a separate and distinct identity, and comparing may have its positive points (my baby is heavier; my baby is more alert), there may also be drawbacks for those who do not feel that their babies compare. Take the time to explore what you do share: the loss of the pregnancy, the trauma of the birth, and many of the other experiences of the NICU. Finding someone who can understand based on their own personal experiences will give you a connection, an outlet, and appreciation for the triumphs that you have already achieved in parenting your preemie.

Spirituality is an option for many, and you may find that while you have never been spiritual in the past, a faith-based method of support may be comforting to you. Belief in a higher power, no matter your religion, can offer comfort and faith. Try speaking to your pastor, rabbi, or other clergy member about your thoughts. Almost all hospitals, in this day and age, have a social worker, volunteer clergy, or other member of a support team.

During trying times, many families find that the experience of a traumatic birth or serious illness can cause them to question their beliefs (Why did God do this to me? How can God be so cruel to cause a child pain?). The birth of the child is a miracle in and of itself. Sometimes there are no answers to how or why things happen. Faith-based support can offer you a focus on the future and a way to view the miracles that occur every day in life. There is nothing that we can do to change what has happened in the past, so why dwell on it? The word *miracle* is common in the English language; we recognize that they exist. Pray for a miracle. Do not be afraid to explore your spiritual side; connections are sometimes made in the most difficult of situations.

Journaling is also a great source of self-support. Just taking the time to put your innermost thoughts and feelings into words can help you to identify your fears and your hopes. Journaling can also help you to identify your role in parenting your preemie. Finally, journaling gives you the opportunity to review your thoughts and feelings at a later time. It is not uncommon to experience the same emotions in a different set of circumstances.

MASTERING THE SKILLS OF PATIENCE AND CALM

You have been able to stop and identify your real fears versus the irrational fears. Now how do you keep the irrational fears and thoughts that occur with them from reentering your mind? The answer is that you cannot. The trauma of your experience will continue, and the roller coaster of emotions that are an intricate part of parenting in the NICU will not subside. However, if you find that these self-destructive, irrational fears are recurring, you might consider trying a self-help technique referred to as "thought stopping." Thought stopping is one of the oldest cognitive techniques and is still practiced widely. The technique was first introduced by a Mr. Bain in 1928 and was later adapted by Joseph Wolpe. Thought stopping is primarily used in cases involving compulsive behavior. However, it is indicated when specific thoughts or images are repeatedly experienced as painful or when these thoughts lead to a less than pleasant emotional state.

You have already identified your fears and rationalized which fears are realistic. You still find yourself thinking about your fears, despite the fact that the rational side of you tells you that it is wasteful thinking. Try interrupting these thoughts with pleasant thoughts. Think of your favorite place, sight, or sound. Some people have found that it is helpful to forcefully tell themselves, Stop! or to pinch or flick themselves before beginning to switch thoughts. Another brief technique to help you in stopping these intrusive thoughts is to focus on your breathing. Controlled breathing is a common technique intended to empty your mind and place your focus on inhaling and exhaling. Try taking five deep breaths; place your hand across your abdomen to make sure that you are extending it to its fullest potential. As you exhale, count one, and as you reach five, you should begin to feel your body relaxing. Each person has a significantly different level of tolerance, so you may find that it takes more than five breaths to clear your mind. If you still find that these fears are overwhelming and causing you marked distress, you should consider talking to a professional.

FACING THE DIFFICULT DECISIONS

Unfortunately, many of us have to make difficult decisions regarding our babies that can have long-term effects. The most important aspect of this decision-making process is that you be a part of it. There are many interventions that your child will need, and the doctors will not consult you or ask your opinion. Other courses of treatment, however, can be administered at different levels, including life-saving measures. Your decision will be taken into consideration on how aggressively to pursue these options. Part of the difficulty in making these hard decisions is that there is no guarantee of the outcomes. Medicine is a science, and there is much that is unknown.

The doctors can provide you with details of potential risks, benefits, statistics, and a wealth of information that will still end in you and your family having to live with your choice. It is strongly recommended that you get a second opinion on any type of decision regarding the long-term well-being of your child. This can add to your confusion as you will find that not all medical providers will have the same opinion. The three things that you want from your medical provider are (1) the most current information about the condition that your child has; (2) the medical and ethical issues presented to you; and (3) assurance that all the pros and cons of each choice have been explained to you. Once you have grappled with the decision, gone back and forth a hundred times, and feel committed to your choice, you will have to live with your decision.

If your decision does not have the outcome you anticipated, you must know that you did what you felt was in the best interest of your child based on the information that was provided to you. You can also take comfort in knowing that medical providers have an ethical obligation to also provide care that is in the best interest of the baby. If your decision was not based on sound judgment, the doctor could have overridden your decision. Try not to second-guess yourself on any decisions. In time you will come to accept the choices you made.

You will still experience grief over the outcome of your decision, but you will see a light at the end of the tunnel.

Some of us are further faced with difficult decisions even after we leave the NICU. Those preemies who will require continued medical care—and choices of who will care for them—present further considerations. Trust the same instincts you had in the NICU; you will have gained a great deal of confidence by the time you have left it. Use your better judgment to make an informed decision about the needs of your child. There are federally funded programs for premature infants until the age of three, which can help you and your family care for your baby.

NICU MONSTERS: COMMON NICU EQUIPMENT

Being able to recognize some of the more common equipment in the NICU will help to alleviate your fears of the unknown. This list, while not all inclusive, provides you with a basic understanding.

Billi-Light/Phototherapy/Billi-Blanket

Some premature infants are born with or develop a condition called jaundice. The condition will cause your baby's skin to appear yellow in color. These babies are commonly treated with billi-lights. The blue florescent lights are place over your baby and are extremely bright. Since the baby's eyes can be sensitive to the brightness, they are usually covered by eye protectors. While treating the jaundice, the babies are usually dressed in only a diaper. A billi-blanket provides the same source of phototherapy but does not require the baby to wear the protective eye patches.

Bulb Syringe

This is a soft-tipped rubber bulb, used to manually suction secretions from the infant's mouth and nose. Parents are taught how to use this syringe before discharge.

Cardiorespiratory Monitor/Heart-Respiratory Monitor

This is the most common piece of equipment in the NICU. This monitor is used to monitor the heartbeat and breathing of your baby. Usually, there are three electrodes placed in various spots on your baby's chest and abdominal area. From the electrical signals the cardiorespiratory monitor is able to pick up the rate and regularity of the respirations. Alarms are set on these monitors at certain levels to indicate abnormal breathing or heart rate.

Continuous Positive Airway Pressure (CPAP)

The continuous positive airway pressure (CPAP) machine is a soft plastic tube that is placed in the baby's nostrils to deliver oxygen when he continues to have difficulty keeping his lungs fully inflated. The CPAP provides just enough air to keep the baby's lungs expanded and allows him to breath independently.

Gel Cushion

This is used for developmental positioning and support.

Giraffe

This is a specialized modern bed that looks like a spaceship and is a combination of a radiant warmer and an isolette. It is usually reserved for micropreemies or for preemies that require critical care. This piece of equipment can also provide a source of moist heat and has a built-in scale.

Isolette

This piece of equipment was formerly referred to as an "incubator." This is an enclosed, quiet space that allows your baby to rest. The inside of the isolette can be heated to help regulate the baby's body temperature.

IV Pumps

These are commonly seen in many areas of a hospital. This piece of equipment delivers fluid though plastic tubing into the baby's body. The fluid is carefully regulated, as is the site where the fluids enter the body. There are many different sizes and shapes of IV pumps, but they all provide the same service.

Nasal Canula

A nasal canula is plastic tubing with two prongs that extend into the baby's nostrils for the delivery of oxygen. It fits around the baby's ear and across the cheek.

Open Crib/Open Bed

This the last bed your baby will see before he goes home. This is a open bed, similar to a radiant warmer but without the overhead arm. A preemie placed in this bed must be able to maintain his body temperature without additional heat sources.

Pulse Oximeter

A pulse oximeter is used to measure the amount of oxygen in your baby's blood. It is a small red light encased in tape. The tape is wrapped around your baby's finger or toe to measure the level of oxygen. The location where the light is placed will shift from time to time.

Medication Pumps

These pumps are similar to an IV pump and administer medications to the baby through the IV. These pumps are usually attached to the IV, and the medication pumps double-check that the appropriate amount of medication is being administered.

Radiant Warmer

This is usually the first bed that your baby will have and is most often temporary. The last trimester is usually when a baby gains the most body weight. Premature babies are born with little body fat and have difficulty maintaining their temperatures. The radiant warmer consists of an overhead arm with electric heating elements that face down on the baby as he lies there. The baby will have a thermostat attached to his body to keep the baby's body temperature regulated. The glass shelves on the side are low enough to allow easy access to the baby but are tall enough to prevent drafts. There is also a scale built into the bed, which allows the baby to be weighed without disruption.

Scale

This piece of equipment, while larger than what you have on the bathroom floor, performs the same task: taking the weight of the baby. The weight of your baby is critical to his development and well-being. The baby's weight is usually taken at the same time each day with the same scale for the most accurate reading. Any equipment or diapers are also taken into consideration. This scale is also sometimes used to measure the weight of a diaper. Weighing diapers ensures that your baby is urinating and having bowel movements regularly and at the proper level based on his intake.

Temperature Probe

This probe is connected to the baby's skin, usually by tape. The probe is most commonly attached when the baby is in a radiant warmer or isolette.

Thermometer

This piece of equipment is vital to the NICU staff and comes in may different sizes, shapes, and models. All thermometers do essentially the same thing, which is to measure your baby's temperature. They are similar to a thermometer that you would buy to use at home.

Ventilator

Ventilators are reserved for the most critical and sick patients. If your baby is on a ventilator, then your baby needs assistance to breathe. There are many different types on the market, but the ventilator provides the breath for your baby when he is too sick or ill to breathe himself. The ventilator inflates and deflates the lungs.

THEY CAN HELP YOU

Health care providers are faced with difficult life and death situations every day. There have been many in-depth debates, controversies, and books that address the subject of ethics as they relate to the medical profession. Unfortunately, doctors have to make difficult decisions on a daily basis. Since each decision is so distinct and critically important to the parents, most doctors will take the approach of consistency to each situation, being careful not to judge you, your family, or your ability to care for your infant. With that in mind, and since the patient—the baby—is unable to make his wishes known, a doctor will consider (1) what is in the best interest of the child, (2) the quality of life for the child, and (3) whether continued support is futile. While as a parent, you also are thinking of these issues, your approach is much more emotional and sometimes clouded by fear. Recognize that whether your decision is to provide or not provide treatment to your child, your decision can have long-term effects. Your medical providers are there to help you make informed decisions. If you do not feel that you are getting the answers you need, consult with the hospital about other options available to you. Some hospitals have special teams to review serious medical decisions. There are also review boards if you find that you are in disagreement with the course of treatment being provided to your child. These situations are not commonplace as NICU providers take great pride in supporting not only the babies, but the families in the NICU.

There are many different practitioners available to parents for questions and concerns. Knowing which provider is tasked with each aspect of your baby's care may help you in directing your questions to the appropriate source.

Audiologist—Medical professional who performs hearing screenings.
Endocrinologist—A medical doctor who specializes in hormonal deficiencies.
Cardiologist—A medical doctor specializing in conditions of the heart.
Gastroenterologist—A medical doctor specializing in intestinal and nutritional problems.
Neonatologist—A pediatrician with special training in newborn intensive care and development.
Nephrologist—A medical doctor specializing in problems related to the kidney.
Neurologist—A medical doctor specializing in disorders of the nervous system.
Nurse-practitioner—A registered, licensed nurse who has been further trained to provide duties similar to that of the neonatologist.
Pulmonologist—A medical doctor specializing in the lungs and breathing issues.
Occupational therapist—A licensed provider specializing in the developmental issues and requirements for proper growth.
Ophthalmologist—A medical professional trained in treatment of the eyes.
Pediatrician—A medical doctor specially trained to deal with the medical issues of children and adolescents.
Physical therapist—A licensed professional trained in the quality of movement, physical agility, and ability.
Respiratory therapist—A licensed professional trained in the care and management of oxygen, breathing equipment, and respiratory therapy.

For further information about health care providers that may be participating in your baby's medical care, you should consult the primary neonatologist.

Chapter 5

Jealousy

We have all heard of Shakespeare's "green-eyed monster"—jealousy. We hear in the media, see in television programming, and have a general sense of what the emotion is from our own personal experiences. Jealousy is most commonly associated with intimate relationships: husbands jealous of wives, girlfriends jealous of boyfriends (or vice versa), and any other combination of relationships that may exist. Jealousy is defined as an emotion by one person who perceives that someone else is getting something that the first person wants. In the case of a premature infant the desire can be the something that is wanted: attention from the baby, attention from your spouse or significant other, or attention from your other family members.

Someone in your family at some point during your ongoing journey of parenting a premature infant will perceive a threat to his relationship with you. A mother may perceive a threat from a nurse in that the baby responds better to the nurse; a child may perceive the threat of a new baby taking all the attention; a father may perceive his wife as more concerned with the baby than with the spousal relationship. The possibilities for jealousy that exist in this emotional journey are endless; how you choose to respond to and work through the jealousy will be important in defining future relations.

It is important to define the differences between jealousy and envy. The more ability you have to identify your emotions, the more you are able to clarify them in your mind. Identification of the emotion will also make you better equipped to process and work through it. Envy involves wishing to get what one does not have. Jealousy is wishing to keep what one has. Envy is usually targeted toward something specific. Jealousy sometimes cannot even be defined. Although it may seem as if you are envious of what you do not have with the baby or others at the time, you really already have these relationships. They just need fine-tuning. You must establish the core belief that there is a bond between you and the baby, you and your spouse, and other familial relationships that have brought you to this point. You already have a strong relationship with your baby, whom you nurtured during your pregnancy. This relationship is significant and cannot be replicated by anyone else.

Jealousy will produce a number of physical and emotional signals that can cause significant difficulty in relationships if they are left to linger. Since there are a number of other emotions that are experienced as a result of jealousy, they also can create conflict in your relationships. Some of the other emotions that are associated with jealousy include anger, fear, hurt, anxiety, agitation, sadness, paranoia, depression, coveting, feeling powerless, feeling inadequate, or just feeling left out.

While jealousy is defined as an emotion itself, the most common underlying emotion in jealousy is fear: Fear of the unknown, fear of change, fear of losing power and control, or fear of loss and abandonment are all reflected in jealousy. It is also a reflection of your own insecurity about your worthiness or adequacy to accomplish what needs to be done.

COMPARING MY BABY

You will compare your baby to others in the NICU. You cannot help yourself, and it is nothing to be ashamed of. Maybe the baby next to yours is not as sick, or is heavier, or interacts with his mother more. Rest assured that as much as you long for your baby to be "like that," that mother at some point wished the same thing. You may even go so far as to wish you had that baby. This is, in part, because you have not completed the process of bonding with your baby.

None of us wishes to experience trauma, sadness, or heartache. The less anxiety we feel about our perceived situation, the more comfortable we are physically and mentally. When you are in the NICU, with the tiniest of humans, every ounce, every movement, every beep makes a difference. The emotions associated with comparing can be more attributed to envy than they can to jealousy. You are longing for something that you do not have. It is important to keep in mind that a preemie is a masterpiece not yet completed. What you do not have, what you envy in the baby next door, will come to you in time.

WHO IS THE MOTHER?

You walk into the NICU, and your nurse is holding the baby, feeding the baby, and looking into his eyes—a chore that not many people would have been allowed to do this early had your baby been full term. Under no circumstances would it be done by a total stranger. This stranger not only has taken away your duties as a mother, but she is now going to tell you when you can touch your baby, hold your baby, feed your baby, and even soothe your baby. While the rational side of your mind recognizes that at this time, the nurse's job of keeping your baby healthy is priority, at the same time, her care of your baby causes you to feel that you are not making a contribution. You are jealous of what you perceive to be a developing relationship that belongs to you. Keep in mind that while the medical staff is there to provide support and supervision in caring for the baby, they are not teaching you how to be a good mother. They are teaching you how to be a substitute medical provider. The feelings of love and the comfort you bring to the baby will come from inside; your voice, your smell, and your touch arise from the motherly instincts that come naturally and cannot be substituted. Even if you find yourself still slightly detached from the baby, your baby recognizes you and feels comfort in your presence.

For most parents, this is their first experience with a NICU, and ignorance about all the medical jargon leads to frustration and feelings of helplessness. You have to be able to recognize and desensitize through exposure those things that produce jealousy and revise your thought process as it relates to these events. You must learn to accept the jealousy as normal and as an exaggerated response to a stressful and emotionally charged change that is occurring in your life: becoming parents to a baby that is less than the image of perfect.

I CANNOT BE THERE ALL THE TIME

Learning to accept the jealousy is a critical component in coming to terms with the health care providers who are caring for your baby. As much as you would like to be in the NICU every waking moment for your baby, it is impossible and unfair to your family. Not being able to be in the NICU to care for your baby every minute of every day furthers your resentment and jealousy of the health care providers that are at the hospital. In the back of your mind, you fear that they might see "the first" something, whether it be a coo or a smile.

There may be other times when you just feel that you cannot muster the energy to go to the NICU, even if it is around the corner. Whether you want to go to the hospital or not evokes a guilty conscience for the perceived neglect of your baby. If you choose not to go to the hospital, the neglect of your baby weighs on your mind; if you choose to go, the neglect of your other obligations feels overwhelming. You have to strike a balance between the two. Remember that your hardest critic is yourself. No one will find fault with you for taking a breather.

You think the world should stop, or maybe you just do not care what happens outside of the NICU. Realistically, you know you have to find a way to balance your home, work, and family while adjusting to life in the NICU. You will probably have time off from work, and no one will care if the housekeeping is not kept up, but since the NICU is generally a long-term facility, bills will have to be paid and laundry will have to be done. If there are other children in the home, their needs will have to be tended to as well. School projects, homework, and social activities will continue to be a priority for other children. A child cannot recognize the magnitude of a premature baby in the NICU and will expect his life to run as usual.

I MISS MY FAMILY AND THEY MISS ME

You are torn in two directions while trying to strike a balance. There may be children or other loved ones at home that are feeling the loss of your presence. Your baby will not be verbalizing his need for you in the NICU, but your maternal instincts will not allow you to walk away. Your family misses you as much as you miss your family. The loss of your presence and routine has impelled each member of your family to take on new roles and responsibilities.

While your spouse is most likely sharing the responsibilities of caring for the baby, the home, and all of the other daily obligations, your relationship may be strained solely by the difference in the way men and women process stress. Sometimes the marriage stress may not even be present in the form of fighting, yelling, or sulking, as most would expect. Most men have been taught self-assertiveness and may feel belittled by admitting to stress. Men tend to view talking as "feminine" and will sometimes withdraw, knowing that their spouses may have information about their weaknesses or fear of being unable to effectively communicate their own feelings. If the stress is not expressed in the form of anger, it can also be expressed in the form of social isolation. Men traditionally view themselves as providers, protectors, and disciplinarians, and their role models were their own fathers. A great deal of stress is harbored when they have no control over a situation. As the loss of control increases, as does the level of stress. The "strong male role" is compromised because they no longer can protect or provide for their children. They also find stress in the inability to comfort their own concerns while at the same time addressing their spouses. There is no adjustment period available because the demands and outcomes are unpredictable. Leaning on each other, even when the conversations may at times feel one sided, you know that in the end you both want the best possible outcome for your baby. The best advice is to keep the lines of communication open. Women tend to have an easier time expressing their hopes, fears, and dreams for a positive outcome. Be patient with your spouse you have the same goals. Some of the warning signs that your relationship may need additional help in processing this experience together are

☑ if either finds himself or herself becoming angry or defensive when talking about difficult situations
☑ if either is openly and overly critical of the other
☑ if either retreats and isolates himself or herself from the relationship
☑ if either finds it difficult to share the emotions of the experience for fear of the response he or she might receive
☑ if either finds himself or herself leaning on others in an effort to compensate for what he or she feels is missing from the other.

Seeking professional help may not only help with the marital conflicts, but it may also be beneficial for you as individuals in healing the wounds from the trauma of the experience. If you have other children, a united front will also give them a sense of comfort.

How your other children respond to having a sibling in the NICU will have a great deal to do with their age. Honesty and reality, in small doses, can help children of any age adjust to the traumatic event. While younger children have difficulty understanding the concept of hospitalization, their more immediate concern is the loss of your presence. Older children, while they miss the parental unit, experience both concern for the baby and concern over how the family unit is changing. Be honest with your children—they have big ears, so better they hear things from you and your spouse than from someone else. You will only add to the worry and apprehensiveness if they feel as if something is being kept from them. Your children will experience some of the same emotions you feel: anger, jealousy, and guilt. Communicate with them about their feelings and make them aware that you have similar feelings. Do not be alarmed if your children do not respond in a loving and supportive manner. Depending on the situation and the child, you may see behaviors in your child that introduce themselves as rejection, acting out, or regressing. The best thing that you can do for your children is to be there for them. The small but familiar gesture of making breakfast, taking them to school, or tucking them in gives children a sense of confidence that things will return to normal.

Communicate to your children that the baby will not always be in the hospital and that when he is bigger and stronger, he will come home to be with the family. While they may accept that you are spending time with the baby in the hospital, your children may experience anxiety or jealousy over the thought of the baby's homecoming. Since your children will more than likely not be allowed in the NICU, or only on a very limited basis, it is essential that they view the baby as real. While they know that you have had a baby, it is difficult for them to grasp the concept of the child as a living, breathing human. You can make the baby more alive to them by showing them pictures, talking about the baby, or having them create artwork for the baby. These may be many of the same things you did as you were preparing for the birth.

A GRANDPARENT'S PAIN

Grandparents deserve a special mention in the family unit, and their emotions are deeply affected by the birth of a premature grandchild. They are not only faced with the concerns of the grandchild but also with their concerns for their own children, the parents. You grew up with this family, so you probably have a good idea of how they will handle a stressful situation. Some grandparents withdraw. They withdraw out of their owns fears, not knowing what to do and fearing intruding in an already stressful situation. Others grandparents may go to the extreme and try to take over the situation, whether at home or in the hospital. Be open with your parents about the baby's medical condition and your own needs. Your parents know you as well as you know them, and it causes them great pain to see their own children suffering. While their attempts to help may be frustrating and maybe intrusive, they have the best interests of you and your baby at heart.

EVERYONE I KNOW IS PREGNANT

It always seems that when a women is pregnant, she becomes aware of just how many pregnant women there are out there. It seems as if everyone is pregnant when you are pregnant. This may be true—you may be at an age when most of the friends that you socialize with are in the same life stage of beginning their families. It may not be true, and you just may be more aware of pregnant women because you share a commonality with them. Whichever is the case, either now or in the future, you will know someone who is pregnant, and you will feel jealous or, in this case, maybe more envious.

What is interesting is that friends who are aware of what you have gone through or are going through may have their own guilty feelings about their pregnancies, at least when it comes to sharing the details with you. They may feel that if they say the wrong thing or express joy, you would feel insulted or hurt, which is why, with friends as much as with your family, it is essential to share your emotions. Someday you will be leaving the NICU and reconnecting with the life that you had. You will want to maintain friendships and bonds that existed before. If your friends feel uncomfortable or awkward, a distance will be created. Most of your friends and family are there for you. They want to help you in any way they can and just do not know how. The reality is that what you probably need are the most simplistic of life's chores—laundry, cooking, cleaning, picking up the kids, and so on. Your family and friends are not mind readers, and the imposition you feel in asking for assistance will probably come as more of a relief to you and your friends.

A NOTE TO MY FRIENDS

What do parents wish others understood about the birth of their premature babies?

Adapted with Permission from "Wish upon a Star" by Elaine Grier, Roman's Mom

I wish you would not be afraid to speak my child's name and talk of him without the tone of sympathy, sorrow, and pity in your voice. My child lives and is important, and I need to celebrate his existence. If I cry or get emotional when we talk about my child, I wish you knew that it is not because you have hurt me; the fact that my child is struggling and is not quite perfect has caused me tears. You have allowed me to cry, and I thank you. Crying and emotional outburst are healing.

I wish you would recognize my child's birth with your words and actions and not center on his chance for survival, disabilities, and a "normal" life.

I will have emotional highs and lows, ups and downs. I wish you would not think that if I have a good day, my pain is all over, or that if I have a bad day, I need psychiatric counseling.

I wish you knew that the birth of a preemie is different from other pregnancies and births and must be treated differently. It is tragedy and celebration, fear and joy, gain and loss, among so many other things. I wish you would not compare it to your pregnancy or to the sickness of a parent, a spouse, or a child.

Being a premature parent is not contagious, so I wish you would not shy away from me and my baby.

I wish you knew that all of the "crazy" grief reactions I am having are in fact very normal. Depression, anger, frustration, hopelessness, and the questioning of values and beliefs are to be expected following the birth of a premature baby.

I wish you would not expect my pain and healing to be over in six months. The first year is going to be very hard for us. I will be raising a child whose early life is very different from full-term babies. I will be coming to terms with many emotions. I will be mourning many losses, even though I gained a beautiful baby. As with alcoholics, I will never be "cured" or a "former preemie parent," but will forevermore be parent to a preemie.

I wish you understood the physical reactions to the pain of emotions such as the ones I feel now. I may gain or lose weight, sleep all the time or not at all, develop a host of illnesses, and be accident prone, all of which may be related to my emotions.

Our child's birthday, his due date and homecoming, and those other anniversaries are important times for us. We may celebrate but also mourn and relive the pain. I wish you could tell us that you understand that we are dealing with lots of tough emotions. Do not try to coerce us into being cheerful, even though that is what is expected.

It is normal and good that most of us reexamine our faith, values, and beliefs after a preterm birth. We question things we have been taught all our lives and hopefully come to some new understanding with our God. I wish, if I am one who must tangle with my religion, that you would let me do so without feeling guilty.

I wish you would not offer me drinks or drugs. These are just temporary crutches, and the only way I can get through this process of healing is to experience it. I have to hurt before I can heal. If I need help from counselors and antidepressants, please help me get it.

I wish you understood that having a premature baby changes people. I am not the same person I was the moment before my child arrived and never will be that person again. If you keep waiting for me to "get back to my old self," you will stay frustrated. I am a new creature with new thoughts, dreams, aspirations, values, and beliefs. Please try to get to know the new me—maybe you will like me still.

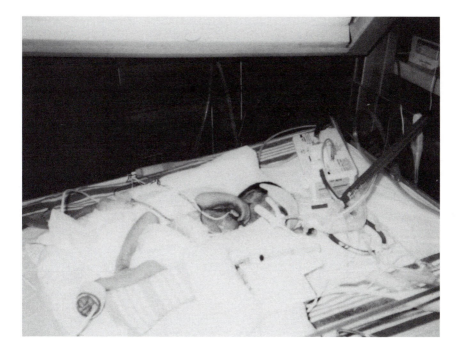

Chapter 6

Going Home Alone

Since most preemies stay in the NICU until their original due dates, the time they are in the hospital can span from 10 to 12 weeks, more or less. The average stay for a mother who has had no serious complications is usually no more than a week. This means that there will come a time when you must leave your baby in the hospital and return home without him. This can be an extremely overwhelming time for a mother. You have come to accept the fact that your baby was born prematurely and have begun to work through the emotions associated with the experience. You are still in the healing stages when they tell you it is time to go home. Your life has been completely turned upside down in the previous weeks, and some parents may have not ever considered the possibility that they would have to leave their baby. Many mothers have said that they just assumed they would stay with the baby. The thought of leaving the baby compounds the anxiety, guilt, and fear that is already being felt.

You cannot comprehend how the hospital staff could ever suggest that you leave your baby when he is in an intensive care unit. You consider the insensitivity of those asking you to leave as being nothing short of cruel. However, the rational side of you knows that the bed you are occupying could be used for another mother who is about to give birth. The need for the bed coupled with rising health care costs make hospitals quick to ask you to leave. Your insurance carrier will be right behind them.

There are alternatives, especially for those who live a distance from the hospital. Many hospitals have housing on site for a nominal fee or free of charge so that families can get a good night's sleep and a shower. This service is not only for parents of preemies, but also for other families who wish to be close to their loved ones during a serious illness. Talk with the hospital social worker for possible accommodations outside of the hospital while your baby is recovering.

SEPARATION ANXIETY

There is a direct correlation between a mother being separated from her child and the anxiety that she feels. While your baby may be out of sight, he is never out of your mind. In speaking with mothers of babies in the NICU, the two most important things to them were that their babies got better and that they were able to be there for their babies. Since being there for the baby ranks as a priority for most mothers, it is not unexpected that having to be separated from your baby, even just for a brief period of time, would cause additional stress in an already overly stressful situation.

We will talk about stress in greater detail later in this book. What you need to recognize early on is that stress is not only an emotion, but that is has a significant effect on a physical level as well. Stress starts in your brain and sets off an internal alarm that there is a potential threat. This triggers a number of physical reactions, such as a racing heart, sweaty palms, and extreme muscle tension. The potential threat involving separation from your baby is most often a fear of the unknown. A typical example is a new mother who fears leaving her baby with someone other than her spouse for the first few weeks, sometimes even months. We have all heard this scenario and almost expect it from a new mother. This is not because she has rational, valid reasons for fearing something can happen. It is more of an instinctual fear that her baby might need her, and no one else will be able to fill that need other than her. As a parent of a preemie, on the other hand, while you have a valid reason for fearing that something will happen to your baby, you also have to recognize that your baby is in the safest place possible. Not only is your baby safe, but your baby is being tended to by trained medical professionals, who are monitoring every aspect of the baby's health.

If you have been exposed to the NICU at all, you will recognize that it is a ward, a unit, not an individual room. The NICU is a critical care unit, and as with an adult intensive care unit, visitation is limited for the safety of the patients, so bunking in is out of the question. It is not realistic, nor do they make it comfortable for you to spend every waking minute there. This is intentional. Imagine the chaos if every parent of every child was staying in the NICU. While the rational side of your brain recognizes this, you cannot help but say that you still want to stay.

The following is a list of good reasons to leave.

☑ Separation is considered an important part in the developing character of a child. By leaving your baby you are actually teaching your baby memory recall and the ability to recognize someone familiar when you return.

☑ Preemies need sleep, and as the NICU tries to replicate the womb for the baby, it is necessary for the baby to sleep—just as it is necessary for you to sleep. A tired mom is an irritable mom, and your baby will sense your irritability.

☑ There is nothing that you can do. While just being there is essential for the growth and development of your preemie, this does not mean you need to be there every minute. A brief period of time spent alone or with family and friends can have a positive impact on your attitude, which will be felt by your baby. If you cannot get past the feelings that your baby should not be alone, then have your spouse, a friend, or a family member replace you while you take a well-needed rest.

☑ While nothing can take priority over your baby, you have a family that needs you, and you need them. As you go through the emotional roller coaster of parenting a preemie, you will need the support of your family and friends. Do not shut them out.

☑ Being in the NICU every day does not make you a better parent. Even if you are able to go to the NICU every day, you probably will not feel a sense of completeness as a parent. Your biggest wish is for the baby to come home, and that is where you will feel the full responsibility of parenthood.

☑ Absence makes the heart grow fonder. You will begin to see when you return to the NICU how your baby responds differently to you than to the nurses. Look for the cues in chapter 7 of recognizing when your baby is pleased.

POSTPARTUM DEPRESSION

Four out of five mothers will be affected by the baby blues. There will also be an additional 10 to 17 percent of mothers who are affected by some other mood or anxiety disorder. There is reason to believe that the additional traumas that you have experienced make you susceptible to something more than just a mild case of the baby blues. You have just had a baby and are experiencing the emotional turmoil that goes hand in hand with a preemie. You have been traumatized by the experience, and you can expect to have periods of depression.

Postpartum depression usually sets in approximately six to eight weeks after the birth of your baby. Postpartum depression is not only an emotional condition but has its etiology in genetics. There are a number of factors that contribute to postpartum depression: family history of depression, chronic sleep deprivation, fatigue, hormonal changes, medical complications, fertility treatments, internalization of criticism, and absence of support from family and friends.

While the baby blues occur usually within 48 hours after delivery and resolves itself within two weeks of delivery, postpartum depression can occur up to two years after delivery. As mental health professionals, it can be difficult to diagnose postpartum depression. Postpartum depression can be deceiving as it can mask itself as a number of other anxiety disorders. Postpartum depression is a serious disorder and should not be taken lightly. Undiagnosed, this disease can result in debilitating results. Postpartum depression can change your personality, your relationships, your spirit, and your goals.

In the case of a woman who has had a premature baby, it can be difficult to distinguish baby blues from depression or even generalized anxiety. The reasoning behind this is when a woman has had a full-term birth, there is an expectation of happiness, joy, and an overall positive experience. When a women does not feel these emotions, she may began to question herself. While a woman may fear exposing feelings of sadness, anxiety, and concentration, she cannot deny to herself that they exist. It is hoped that they will seek attention if for no other reason than that they are not "supposed" to feel this way by society's standards.

A woman who has had a premature baby does not have the happy ending to pregnancy that we all anticipate at the end of nine months. The baby is in an intensive care unit, and her feelings of sadness and anxiety are expected. This is the way society expects you to react. It is considered a norm. The question becomes, how do you recognize when your feelings are something more than a natural expression to an immediate stressor? How do you know when the feelings are too intense and lasting too long? Knowing yourself is the answer.

Women in general are strong, multitasking, and independent. While in some cases you may portray a more passive exterior, internally, you have a survival instinct that will present itself even in the most stressful of situations. When depression sets in, a sense of hopelessness passes over you, like a fog passing through your brain. You may fear telling anyone of the symptoms you recognize as not being yourself. You just try to shake off the feelings, and when you cannot, it causes you additional anxiety. Some of the symptoms may include

☑ a sense of inadequacy as a mother and wife
☑ difficulty sleeping
☑ lack of interest in the baby

☑ difficulty concentrating
☑ daily crying
☑ a lower than normal level of functioning, including personal hygiene
☑ mood swings
☑ zoning out.

Trust your instincts when it comes to your thoughts and expressions of emotion. You know better than anyone what is the norm for you. If your feelings continue past two weeks or seem to be intensifying, seek professional assistance. There is no test for postpartum depression, but there are screening measures that can be performed by professionals in the field of mental health.

If you feel uncomfortable seeking out the assistance of a mental health professional, discuss your symptoms with your doctor. However, it is important to note that most doctors recognize that your hormones are affected after pregnancy. Being that your hormones are off, a physician may not recognize the severity of your symptoms. It is recommended that if you are still experiencing the symptoms described after you have taken the course of treatment prescribed to you by your physician, you take the next step and consult a mental health professional.

SELF-TALK: REALITY MUST RULE

The following list of exercises is intended to help relieve the anxiety and fear that you feel in leaving your baby alone in the NICU. The first rule to remember is reality. You cannot set goals based on unrealistic fears; you must recognize what is reality and what is overactive anxiety. Without distinguishing the two, it will be difficult to feel any sense of security in the decisions you make.

In recognizing reality, you understand that the real fear you have is being afraid that something will happen if you leave the baby alone in the NICU. Keep in mind that the word *alone* means without family, not without the respiratory therapists, neonatologists, nurse-practitioners, nurses, and other medical professionals who monitor the NICU 24 hours a day, seven days a week. Imagine your worst fear because whether you want to admit it or not, your worst fear is not that the baby will cry or spit up, it is that something serious will happen to your baby. This has to do with catastrophic thinking. In most circumstances you would avoid or try to steer your mind away from catastrophic thinking.

This is the one exception where flooding yourself with worry actually might be beneficial for you in a number of ways, now and as you proceed on this journey. For the purposes of learning to adapt to the anxiety you feel when you are separated from your baby, flooding yourself with your worry may actually cause you to adapt to the anxiety, thus making it less painful. Before you decide to flood yourself with worry, you must first define the worries that are realistic.

List your worries—are they mistakes the staff will make? Are they physical body failures your baby might have? Are they worries that your baby will be alone or not feel loved? Are you afraid the hospital will have a fire?

Once you have established what the worries are, they become more structured and easier to manage. List every worry, from the most serious to the most minor. Now take the time to put them in some sort of order, from most serious to least serious. An example might be the following.

I worry that the baby will have a seizure.
I worry that my baby will cry and no one will hear.
I worry that no one will turn his music back on.
I worry that he will not feel loved.

When you are able to identify what you are worried about, you are able to fix conclusively on what the worry is and how important it is to you. This is a more structured format than worrying about abstracts. The more worries you discover in an unstructured frame of mind, the less likely you are to focus on resolving them.

Once you have established what the worries are autonomously, take each worry and assess the reality of it. On the basis of what you know as fact, not perception, could it happen? While you may be able to assess a preponderance of the worries for validity, when it comes to the medical possibilities, you may find yourself thinking in worst case scenarios simply because you are so uneducated in the medical world. A suggestion may be to ask the medical staff to put the risks for your child into percentages. They cannot give you a guarantee, but most of the medical complications that you find yourself worried about can be put into percentages. A percentage is something you can relate to, for example, 50-50, 70-30. You can also take comfort in knowing that the medical staff in the NICU will let you know when to be concerned.

If your worry is realistic and can happen, then worry about it in the worst possible scenario first. Take time to sit down and worry about it; think of all the possible scenarios how it could happen. What could happen? Who would be there? What would be the outcome? What would you do? Even if you find that your anxiety level is high, continue to think about it until you can think about it no more. You should find that the more you worry, the less anxiety you have toward the worry.

My baby has a seizure and no one is around, and he falls out of the isolette and . . .
My baby cried and no one heard him; he got so worked up that . . .
My baby's music went off and no one checked him all night, so they never realized that . . .
My baby was sad and alone; no one looked at him, touched him, or held him the entire time I was gone, and this . . .

Once you have worried to the point that you can think of no further scenarios or possibilities, take time to relax, unwind for 15 minutes, release the tense muscles, take deep breaths, and calm your mind. Think positive thoughts. Before you can focus on the next step, you will want to have eased the anxiety from your body.

The second step to getting your worries under control is to take the same worries that you just agonized over and think of all the possible alternatives to them. What else could happen? How could it happen? Who would be there? Remember that this is not your worst possible scenario; this is an alternative theory. Your alternative worries might be the following.

My baby has a seizure and the medical staff is able to control it, and they contacted me immediately and . . .
My baby was crying; the nurse came over to soothe him and he . . .
My baby's music stopped playing, and when the nurse came to check him, she turned it back on; that made . . .
My baby was cuddled as he was fed by his night nurse, and he . . .

Most people will find that the most serious of worries are exaggerated, and given the facts, the more likely outcome will be your alternative theory. After you have established your alternative theories, determine if there is anything that you could do to change your worry. Would none of it have happened if you were there? If you were there, would it make a difference? If your worry is a medical condition, you need to remind yourself that you have no control over the fluctuations of a preemie's health.

Even after you have taken the time to analyze your worries, you might still find that you feel uncomfortable leaving your child. If this is the case, then you may want to consider having someone that you trust there when you cannot be. You may find that you have to take baby steps before you can comfortably leave your child. Each person has a distinctly different level of comfort, and you have to do what is comfortable for you.

Some women feel confident in the staff at the NICU and are able to leave their babies for extended periods of time; others have to adjust out of necessity. However, that does not mean that you will not worry about the baby. This formula for assessing and reducing the anxiety associated with your worries can be used even if separation is not the issue. The medical professionals, your family, and even you recognize the need for you and your spouse, as parents, to maintain your strength physically and emotionally. No one will ever fault you for taking time to yourself.

Chapter 7

Baby Time and Bonding

As you have grown up over the years, somewhere in the back of your mind, whether you have been told or you just know, the first few minutes are when you bond with your baby. Despite this common theory, studies have shown that bonding is a process and is not instantaneous. The first few weeks are when families begin the process of bonding. That special bond that no other person can replace takes time and nurturing. As parents of preemies, we can feel that we are missing something special. The maternity leave, the first six weeks when a mother who has had a full-term baby pampers and showers her little one with love, seems so important that even fathers are now being given paternity leave benefits. Many preemie parents lose that six weeks as they are still in the NICU.

As you enter the NICU, you are confronted with a very cold and impersonal atmosphere full of policies and procedures that seem to do nothing but interfere with your freedom to shower your baby with love and attention. It becomes necessary to form the ability look past the atmosphere and to find a way to bond with your baby. The parental attachment that your baby first feels will be your baby's first model for intimate relationships. The parental attachment is so critical that it forms the basis that will assist your baby in fostering a sense of security as well as positive self-esteem in the future. How you respond to your baby will also affect your baby's social and cognitive development. A lack of parental response can cause delayed development, sadness, and in extreme cases, failure to thrive. Your baby will almost instantly be ready to bond without regard for the medical condition. However, sedative drugs can cause your infant's responses to be different than they might be otherwise.

The way that a baby bonds to its parents is different from the way that a parent bonds to their baby. Parents have to overcome such extreme emotions from the trauma of the birth experience, while preemies are just behaving as nature intended. While they can experience stressors and contentment, they have no expectations. For some parents, especially those that are in the environment of the critical unit of the NICU, they may not feel an immediate connection to the child. You had a vision of what your baby was going to look like, and you are thrown into the NICU with a baby that looks drastically different, if not by traits, than by virtue of the equipment that is attached to him. It may take time for you to adjust your mental picture of the baby. Try to focus on your baby's face. This will be the primary tool in communicating with your baby. Bonding with your baby is a very personal and intimate experience, and it will take time to cultivate. There is no magic button to push to feel attached. An obstacle that makes it difficult to bond with your child in the NICU is that many of us bond by routine—touching the baby, holding the baby, changing the baby—and these options may not be available to you.

The NICU offers a support system and will assist you in developing the confidence that you need to bond with your preemie. The medical providers recognize the importance of forming a bond and provide you with the tools to be able to start the process as soon as possible. The hospital staff can assist you in holding and touching your baby and will encourage you to actively bond with your baby. Keep in mind that the nurses and doctors in the NICU are trying to recreate the womb for your baby by swaddling the baby tightly and keeping the baby warm and quiet, just as the baby would have been in the womb. Studies have shown that babies from as early as six months intrauterine are able hear what is going on outside of the womb. That means that your child can hear your voice. You are a significant part of recreating the womb for your baby.

Touching your baby is one of the most important of connections between you and your baby. Touching your baby will not only make the baby real in your mind in such a surreal situation, but it will also enable you and the baby to have a closer relationship. The most common form of touch encouraged by providers in the NICU is called "kangaroo care."

KANGAROO CARE

The term *kangaroo care* refers to holding your undressed baby against your bare chest. This helps in creating a physical and emotional closeness. Also referred to as skin-to-skin care, kangaroo care is encouraged for both parents. There have been impressive studies that show that babies who received kangaroo care showed improved weight gain, improved developmental growth, and more steady heart and breathing patterns, which resulted in shorter hospital stays. Your child can sense the differences in touch, smell, and the sound of voices, so both parents are encouraged to be a part of kangaroo care.

When you are able to provide kangaroo care in the NICU, try to create a sense of privacy for you and your child. While most NICU facilities are set up in a dormitory-like style, they may have drapes, screens, or some other method of isolating an individual isolette. Choose a comfortable chair or position for you. The more at ease you are, the more soothing it will be for your baby. Rocking chairs or chairs with a footrest are commonly used in the NICU. Being in a hospital, there is no shortage of gowns; request a gown, and open it in the front. You want to ensure that every part of your baby is touching your skin, feeling the warmth of your body and recognizing your smell. There is even evidence to support that your baby can sense your emotions, so try to relax. Use guided imagery to a place of peace and comfort for yourself.

Whether you choose to keep your baby diapered is a personal choice, however, for an uninterrupted time with your baby, you may choose to diaper him. Kangaroo care sessions are usually 30 minutes initially and can be up to two to three hours in later sessions. Try to be still and quiet when you are holding your baby; sometimes an immature nervous system can be overwhelmed by a new set of sensations.

Infant massage, as with kangaroo care, forms a closeness to your baby. Massaging an infant is much different from the traditional deep tissue massages you receive as an adult. There is controversy with the concept of massage. Since preemies can be easily overstimulated, massage is not common practice in most NICUs. Consult your health care providers about whether your baby would benefit from infant massage.

MAKING A HOME FOR YOUR BABY

The more comfortable you feel in your environment, the more settled you will begin to feel emotionally. The first step in settling into the NICU is establishing your routine. When will you be there? Are you going to be there for all feedings? Are you going to be there at bath time? You can expect that your baby will sleep most of the time. As your preemie matures, he will begin to establish a state of sleep versus being awake and alert. Try to plan your routine around the times when your baby is alert. Unlike a full-term baby, where the parents try to establish the routine for the baby, preemies get to set the schedule for parents.

Your baby will be able to see and hear you, and preemies very much dislike loud noises, so use a soft, soothing voice with your baby. Some parents are not able to be in the NICU as much as they would like, so as an alternative, they leave voice recordings of themselves singing or telling a story. We have to keep in mind that premature infants can be overstimulated very easily, so too much of any thing may cause your baby to become stressed. Since your baby's eyes may not be completely developed, he will probably be most interested in human faces and patterns of black and white. If you decide to bring in a mobile or other item, be sure that it is new and packaged to prevent bringing germs into the unit.

You can bring in family pictures and name tags for the baby's bed. Ask your health care providers if you can dress your baby and bring in blankets from home. The medical needs of your baby will determine how much the NICU staff will allow you to do. Medical needs must be a priority, and sometimes personal items can interfere with access to your baby. Dressing your baby in your own clothes and swaddling him in your own blankets will help you to connect the child to your family.

HOW CAN I HELP?

You want to hold your baby, feed your baby, change your baby, and play with your baby, but you feel helpless and fearful that you might hurt this frail little baby who has wires and leads that beep and alarm at the slightest movement. There are things that you can do for your baby while your baby is making his home in the NICU. Seek guidance from the medical professionals as your baby is being bathed, changed, and fed by someone every day. Ask how you can help.

Some of the more common ways that you can help include the following.

Taking the Baby's Temperature

While we have become accustomed to associating taking a temperature with being sick, in the NICU the medical professionals are concerned with keeping the baby warm. Since preemies have very little body fat, their temperatures are taken often. The nurse or practitioner will show you how to read and track your baby's temperature.

Changing Diapers

Changing a diaper is not a difficult task to accomplish, however, with all the leads, wires, and other mechanical monsters that can be so intimidating, changing your baby could become difficult. Depending on the gestational age of your baby and his medical condition, you may feel more comfortable having a nurse position your baby first. Keep in mind that while under normal circumstances, you would discard the diaper, it may be important for the nurse to weigh the diaper to make sure that your baby is urinating and having regular bowel movements.

Bathing Your Baby

Most babies in the NICU are given sponge baths because their skin is so sensitive, and these baths usually consist only of warm water. Remember that your baby can sense your touch, and the warm water and sense of touch from you can be beneficial to both you and your baby.

There are a number of other procedures that you might be able to help with, such as changing the tape on a tube, wiping away secretions, and changing the bed blankets. The more care you are able to provide your preemie, the more connected you will feel to him.

Play with Your Baby

As your baby gets older, closer to his due date, you will notice increased periods of alertness. Make this time with your baby interactive, being watchful for cues that your baby might be stressing. Playing with your baby may be as simple as maintaining eye contact, singing softly, showing him pictures of family, or other items. You should be careful to avoid bright pictures, which may be overstimulating.

Bonding is an important area for parents to have an understanding of each other's feelings toward the baby. If one parent has come to acceptance and the other is still healing, the baby can sense the differences in the emotions and will respond to your cues. As your baby grows, it will become more difficult for the baby to know how to respond if one parent treats the child differently. While your initial concerns will be the medical aspects of your baby's health, you need to maintain flexibility to be able to change your connection to the baby as the baby changes. Your baby will not always be in the NICU. Even if your baby will have ongoing difficulties, he will change over time. Do not plan anything; take cues from your baby, respond to him in a positive and soothing manner, and he will respond to you. The interactions will be real and priceless.

KNOW YOUR BABY

Most preemies communicate through physical responses. Knowing when your baby is happy and when your baby is upset or stressed is essential as you begin to define your parenting role. Your baby will communicate to you through three stages: physiology, motor, and state.

Physiology is the way in which the bodily functions of the organs perform their intended tasks. Your baby's organs are premature, as is his central nervous system. Motor are those movements that produce an action, and state is a form of expression. Some cues which may indicate that your baby is experiencing stress include

☑ a change in breathing, which could result in an interruption in heart rate and oxygen levels
☑ a change in color, for example, the nose or lips become pale, a darkness forms around the eyes, or the mouth takes on a blue dusky color
☑ a startle response, for example, your baby becomes stiff, limp, arches his back—commonly referred to as "extension"—or shows tremors, twitches, or frantic movements
☑ a gagging or spitting up response or, the most obvious, a cry
☑ a panicked expression—your baby will look as though he is frightened
☑ avoiding a chance to look at you—your baby may avoid you or a toy, commonly referred to as "gaze averting." Let your baby reestablish the contact.

Some signs that you are positively interacting with your baby follow.

☑ The baby's breathing, heart rate, and oxygen levels are steady.
☑ The baby has an even skin tone, without duskiness.
☑ The baby appears to be relaxed—there is no tension in his muscle tone.
☑ The baby may grasp your finger or curl his own fingers into fists.
☑ The baby may attempt to suck a pacifier, finger, fist, or other object.

Take cues from your baby, as your baby will take cues from you. If you are feeling stressed, your baby may pick up on your tension and exhibit some stressful signs. How you feel and how you respond are equally as important as what you do. If you feel overwhelmed or need a break, take one. Recognizing that you need time to yourself is a sign of emotional maturity that no one will fault you for.

BREAST-FEEDING

Breast-feeding a preemie can be a difficult and, in some cases, impossible task. Depending on the gestational age of the baby, he may not have developed the suck and swallow reflex. This reflex is not usually present until the 34th week. This does not mean that you cannot feed your baby with breast milk. You will find that your medical providers will encourage the expression of breast milk for your baby. A mother's milk is widely accepted as the best possible nutrient for a growing baby, whether the baby is preterm or full term. However, when it comes to a preemie, breast milk is even more advantageous in that it is easier to digest for a preemie because it is loaded with protein, fat, and carbohydrates. In addition, the mother of a preterm infant who expresses her milk will provide the baby with even higher concentrations of nitrogen, sodium, chloride, magnesium, and iron. Breast milk is well known for its intricate part in fighting infection, and preterm breast milk has a higher percentage of the proteins necessary to fight infections. Expressing your milk can be a hassle, but no more of a hassle than preparing a warming a bottle, and the benefits are insurmountable.

Ask your medical providers if there are pumping stations. Many hospitals that encourage breast-feeding will provide you with the equipment necessary for pumping and storage. Your hospital will also have a lactation consultant on staff to help you in mastering the skill of milk expression. If you are unable to feed your baby, your milk will be provided to the baby through a gavage tube: This tube runs through the baby's nose directly to the stomach.

Aside from all the benefits that the breast milk provides to the baby, this is an excellent opportunity for you and your baby to bond. There will come a time when you will have to leave the hospital without your baby. Breast-feeding is a way to feel connected to your baby, even when you are separated. Thinking of your baby when you are expressing milk can actually stimulate the production of milk. The advantage to you as the mother of the baby is that you have a need for this baby to take the milk. Whether the baby is nursing or not, your milk, once in full supply, will need to be let down. Letting down your milk is extremely satisfying.

Some medical providers recommend allowing the baby to play with the nipple after the milk has been expressed. If he has not completely formed the suck and swallow technique, he will find satisfaction in the warmth and may experience the lingering taste of the milk. This is a combination of breast-feeding and kangaroo care. This also is pleasurable for you as stimulation of the nipple by the infant can cause the release of the hormone oxytocin. Oxytocin is called the love hormone because it is also produced during sexual intercourse. Oxytocin causes your uterus to contract and brings a sudden feeling of contentment and pleasure as you feed your baby.

THE BREAST: SEX OR INFANT NOURISHMENT

Some women choose not to breast-feed because they view their breasts as sexual objects and have difficulty viewing them as a form of nourishment for the baby. Women who have experienced an orgasm while breast-feeding have given up breast-feeding because they felt that there was something wrong with them for being sexually aroused. This is common and does not mean that you are aroused by young children.

It is commonly assumed by biologists that the real evolutionary purpose of women having breasts is to attract the male—that breasts are secondary sex characteristics. Some biologists believe that the shape of the female breasts evolved as a frontal match to that of the buttocks. The problem with this theory has been that in many countries around the world, the breast is not sexual. In Africa it is the buttocks; in China it is the foot; and in Japan it is the nape of the neck. Others believe that the human breast evolved in order to prevent infants from suffocating while feeding.

Any part of the female body can be considered an erogenous zone, depending on the sexual template of the individual. To broadly define the breast for the sole purpose of sexuality is like throwing away the baby with the bath water. No matter what the theory, the fact remains that the breast is a milk-producing gland that provides essential nourishment to a preemie.

I AM WORRIED THAT I AM NOT CONNECTING

While it is normal to feel somewhat discombobulated in the NICU, your desire to be a good parent is ingrained in your identity. There are a number of reasons why you may not feel connected to your baby. You may still be recovering from the trauma of the birth. You still may be harboring guilt that you are somehow responsible for your baby's ill health. Your baby's ill health may be causing you to fear becoming attached. The focus on the baby's medical conditions may make the baby seem somehow unreal.

The biggest barrier you will face in becoming connected is convincing yourself that the baby will survive. Once you feel confident in your baby's survival and recognize that your baby is much stronger than he looks, you will be able to move forward. Studies have shown that a baby can sense his mother's reaction and will make attempts to coo or smile in order to get a response.

If you do feel as though you are not bonding with your child the way you believe you should be, talk to the nursing staff. It is nothing to be embarrassed or ashamed of. Many mothers of full-term infants do not feel a connection to their babies immediately. Some of the warning signs that you might not be attaching to your baby and need to seek additional counseling follow.

☑ You feel afraid to comfort or care for your baby.
☑ You feel numb or detached from your baby.
☑ You spend a substantial amount of time with your baby but do not interact with him.
☑ You feel overwhelming fear as it relates to caring for your baby.
☑ You constantly alert medical staff to even minor changes.

The time that you spend in the NICU with your baby will be a long road to adaptation, and the chances are good that you will bring home your infant. As you achieve the medical milestones and participate in the care of your baby, your perceptions of your baby will change.

Chapter 8

Baby's Best Advocate

This baby has been nurtured in your womb for a generous amount of time, and you let nature take its course in bringing about this human being. You have faith in nature since childbirth is "as natural as sunshine." You had this baby before its time and have learned that your body will not allow you to change the course of what is meant to be. However, medical science has progressed over the years and now has the ability to change the course of some of the medical challenges your baby has to face. Some would say changing the course of nature is not always necessarily for the better.

The question that is of most interest to you becomes what part you as a parent play in the course of treatment for your child. While we all respond to stress in different ways, we also all respond to medical afflictions in different ways. Deep in the hearts of all parents, they want what is in the best interest of their babies. The difficulty comes in forming your thoughts into words. In general, the parents of a premature infant can typically fall into one of the following categories when it comes to relating to others in the baby's medical world.

The Hidden or Passive Parent

This is the parent who is either still focused on the trauma of the birth, is not emotionally equipped to deal with the medical aspect of her baby's care, or feels so inept when it comes to dealing with the medical providers that she withdraws and blindly has faith in all the medical decisions that are being made for the baby. This is the parent that would prefer not to know all the details. This parent is easily swayed, has difficulty facing the realities of the baby's condition, and will allow others to violate the rights he has. This parent will avoid offending people at all costs. The passive parent is one who listens to others but may not always hear the information that is being relayed accurately because she feels anxious and unable to concentrate.

The Vocal or Aggressive Parent

This is the parent that most hospitals would prefer not to have. Her own anxiety about the baby's health causes her to be difficult to deal with. She can be demanding, manipulative, and pessimistic. This parent also usually wants unrealistic guarantees about the outcomes of treatment and has a barrage of questions or complaints. Talking with her can be like walking on eggshells, not knowing what response you will get on what day. She tends to blame others when things do not go the way they should. This parent does not react well to suggestions and will not hesitate in violating the rights of others to get what she perceives she is entitled to. The aggressive parent is a poor listener because she finds herself being angry or defensive.

The Concerned or Assertive Parent

This is the most common parent that you will see in the NICU. This parent is the parent who is new to the medical world and whose only concern is what is best for her child here and now. While she cautiously questions the procedures and details of the baby's medical condition, she does not feel confident enough to make suggestions as to other possible treatment plans. She relies on the medical professionals in the NICU to give her the most up-to-date information about her baby. However, if she sees her baby's needs not being met, she will voice her concerns. She feels that she is allowed to say what she feels, stands up for her rights, and sets limits, but she is able to do so without violating the rights of others.

As a medical professional, it is important to identify what type of parent you are dealing with. As a parent, it is important to recognize your own characteristics as they will define how you and the health care providers communicate about your baby's care. While most medical professionals in the NICU recognize the pain and heartache that are associated with having a preemie, they also have to recognize that they are human, and each brings his own personal thoughts and feelings into the relationship. Dealing with families in pain is demanding, and they have to do it every day, but it is not the priority of the health care staff, nor would you want it to be. The staff of the NICU's first priority has to be the baby as a patient.

Many women complain that the staff did not recognize their needs or respond to what was important to them as parents. As you adopt the NICU as your second home, you will find that not everyone will be compatible. You may find it difficult to communicate with people who do not share similar traits or agree with your line of thinking. There will be staff that you feel are more educated, better skilled, more appropriate with their bedside manner, and host of other patterns that can be put into "better" or "worse" categories. We have to put aside our personal feelings and be able to communicate with each and every one of them for the best interests of our babies.

Many families have stated that they felt intimidated by the medical staff, and the doctor in particular. Try not to let this be the case, even though doctors always seem to be so busy and some of us may feel guilty keeping them from saving the next life. You must keep in mind that you are a consumer and that your baby is as important as the next. Spending time with you and your family will make them better doctors.

EFFECTIVE COMMUNICATION SKILLS

You are experiencing one of the most stressful times in your life; how can you possibly be effective in your communication? As you have trouble rationalizing your own thoughts and emotions, you somehow have to find a way to clear the lines of communication with your baby's health care providers. Here are some general suggestions to get the most accurate information from your doctor.

- If you feel overwhelmed by the amount of medical jargon you are exposed to, keep notes or ask another family member to listen extra carefully on your behalf.
- Ask specific questions. If you know some in advance, write them down—there will always be one you forget when the doctor leaves.
- Ask the medical providers for all the pros and cons and any statistics of positive and negative experiences, including their own.
- If you still have questions, the nurses and practitioners are always available in the NICU. If they cannot answer your questions, they will refer you to the appropriate person.
- Paraphrase and repeat the information that has been told to you. This is a check–double check method that ensures that you understand every aspect of what you are being told.

Once you have gathered and assessed all of the information, you will be able to make informed decisions about your baby. When you and your family come to decisions about the care of your baby, your next challenge will be to communicate your thoughts to the medical staff. When you communicate with your medical providers, whether the situation is a serious concern or something minor, how you present yourself will impact the way that they react to you. You should be able to present yourself as confident and self-assured, as you should be—you have just given this baby the gift of life. Be proud. Some other tools to help you in communicating with your health care providers follow.

Be Assertive

Being assertive means that you are confident and self-assured—you are able to stand up for your rights without violating the rights of others. Your requests are fair and specific and are expressed without anger. In order to be assertive with the medical providers, the first thing you must do is get your facts straight. The facts are just that: what you observe, what you see, and what you hear. You may be keeping track through mental notes or a journal; we highly recommend writing things down. Either way, you want to keep track of just the facts as you perceive them. This is not the time to make judgments, place blame, or guess what someone may or may not have intended to do. Your first goal is establishing the facts and expressing them in a very specific and concrete manner. This is difficult as fear may overcome you at times, and your feelings will become hard to separate from facts. If you begin to place blame or judge, you are closing off the possibility for communication and will be less likely to get cooperation from others.

During the second step of learning to be assertive, your goal is to make others aware of how you feel. This does not mean crying uncontrollably or screaming in rage. Expressing your feelings in an overly emotional or extreme way will only make the person you are relating these feelings to defensive. The importance of expressing your feelings is not to make you feel better; the goal is for the other person to understand how his actions, or lack of action, has affected you. If you are composed and specific, your requests will be met with better results.

The third step in being assertive is to make your request fair and possible. You can say, "I want you to make my baby better," and of course, any medical provider would like to answer that question with an affirmative, but he cannot. It is unrealistic and unfair for you to make such a request. The objective in being assertive is to gain a compromise on the way your child is being cared for. You may not like how a particular procedure is administered or are interested in a technique that you read about. There may be a number of reasons for the requests, from personal beliefs to religion and beyond.

How you raise your baby is an individual choice based on your own personal beliefs. Keep this in mind when making requests of health care professionals: While they may agree to meet your requests for certain things, they may not necessarily agree with you. You can change a behavior or the way something is being done without having to change attitudes and feelings. For example, it may be important to you to hold your baby when your baby is being fed, even if the feeding is through a gavage tube. Some medical providers may not see the necessity for holding the baby, and it may be more practical for them to hang the feeding. You, on the other hand, may feel that despite the fact that your baby is not being fed in a traditional manner (bottle or breast), you wish to develop a bond or pattern which you want your baby to expect at feeding times. There is no right or wrong, however, it is a reasonable and fair request, and if it does not interfere with the medical needs of the baby, the request should be able to be accommodated. Another example might be the bathing time of the baby. In most NICUs the babies are bathed in the evening hours, but you may wish this to be done during the day. It may be inconvenient for the nursing staff, but it is not an unreasonable request. There are a number of situations that will arise where you will have the opportunity to express your thoughts in a positive yet assertive manner in order to ensure that you and the medical staff are working together toward providing the best care for your preemie.

Negotiate for What You Want

Different personalities require different approaches. For a more passive parent, one who does not wish to take the chance of offending a medical provider, or anyone else for that matter, you may wish to approach the medical staff with more of a negotiating technique. Negotiating is especially helpful with those headstrong individuals whose ideas and thoughts are as important to them as yours are to you. Negotiation is a way of leveling the playing field so that both provider and patient—in this case, parent—are happy. You must keep in mind when negotiating that policies and procedures dictate what happens in a hospital, not individuals. The fact that we pay thousands upon thousands of dollars to the hospital is an afterthought to the provider, and at this point it may not be on the priority list for you either. If you find yourself negotiating, keep three things in mind: know what you want; state what you want specifically; and listen to the other person's point of view. Understanding the other party's point of view is the key to negotiation. You must have an open mind and use active listening skills, such as paraphrasing or asking for clarification.

Once you understand what you think the other person is trying to say, take that information and formulate a proposal. You must be flexible and fair in your negotiations. Using the above examples, it may not be feasible for the bath time of the baby to be changed every day since the pulmonologist comes on Tuesdays. You might suggest that you be able to bathe your baby three days a week during the day. If you find that in negotiating, your suggestions are met with disapproval, ask for a counterproposal. There is a happy medium for everyone. As practitioners, the medical providers know that it is in the baby's best interest for you as the parents to have an active role in your preemie's care.

Your Body Language

Your body language includes your expressions, tones, and physical movements, which can be characterized as nonverbal communication. According to the research of Albert Mehrabian, PhD, on nonverbal communication, 55 percent of communication is facial expression. That equates to over half of what you say being interpreted by how your facial expressions are perceived.

Albert Mehrabian's research further showed that there are three dimensions of nonverbal cues that we express during conversations. These are immediacy, power, and responsiveness. Immediacy relates to how we space ourselves from each other when we are talking. The theory is rather simplistic in nature and bases itself on the principle that people are attracted to what they like and are turned off by what they do not like. When speaking to a person you like, you will move closer; a person you do not like you will keep a greater distance from.

Power refers to how people dominate or represent themselves in a conversation. Within the first few minutes of a phone conversation a person has a mental image of what you look like, how intelligent you are, how persuasive you will be, and whether or not he is going to listen to you. Power is not something that comes naturally to everyone. Taking into account that you are experiencing an extremely stressful situation, even if you are normally a powerful speaker, you may find yourself mumbling or with a lack of words, or your voice may be in some other form of distress. While you may not be able to control these responses, you can use some of the other techniques mentioned in this chapter to get your message across to others.

Responsiveness refers to how people react to what is being said or how they feel about the person or subject. Being responsive to how someone speaks can be through body signals, such as nodding your head, smiling, shaking your head, or even crossing your arms. Folding your arms across your body is one of the more common signals associated with closed down communication or an unwillingness to participate constructively. The body signals that we project may or may not be consciously done.

READING OTHER PEOPLE

We take the time to recognize our cues and how we respond to others, but how do we recognize the signals that others are projecting toward us? While all the signals mentioned in this chapter can be applied to both the speaker and the intended target of the speech, there are hundreds of other signals and signs that you can look for when speaking with a person. The following, while not an all-inclusive list, will provide you with what we feel are the more common signals that you will come across while you are on the emotional roller coaster of parenting a preemie.

Confident

Leads or dominates the conversation.
Posture is straight; makes consistent, good eye contact.
Good listener.
Walks with confidence.
Willing to engage in conversation.
Stands appropriate distance away; maintains spacing; is not an invader.
Lack of nervousness.

Confusion

Shows signs of frustration.
Repeats himself.
Shows signs of indecision.
Physical movements are repetitive but unstructured.

Defensiveness

Crossed arms, or less commonly, crossed legs.
Hands on hips (more common in women).
No direct eye contact.
Quick breathing or exhaling.
Clenched fists, jaws, teeth, or lips.

Embarrassment

Inappropriate laughter (sometimes called a nervous laugh).
Avoids direct eye contact.
Blushing or turning away.

Fear

Blushing or being flushed.
Gulping or swallowing hard.
Clutching hands or gripping an object tightly (very common in preemie
   moms).
Pacing.
Body stiffness.
Leaning, rocking, or shifting of the upper torso.
Inappropriately grabbing other people.

Worry

Repetitive actions.
Pacing; biting of nails, lips, or hair.
Shaking or fidgeting.
Unable to focus.

One other action that deserves particular attention is the hand-shake. Most of your relationships with the medical staff, or with any new person entering your life, start with a handshake. A handshake for many people, especially men, can define a relationship. I think many women will agree that many men shake the hand of a woman differently than that of a man. It may have to do with culture or up-bringing. That being said, judge your handshakes carefully.

I Am in Charge

This person will try to maneuver his hand on top of yours as soon as the interaction occurs. He wants to be in control and identifies that desire from the beginning of the relationship.

Two Hands Together

When shaking hands, the person places his other hand over yours. This is a very personal greeting, similar to touching the elbow of a person you are shaking hands with. In some cultures it is just as com-mon as a kiss on both cheeks. In other places it could be considered too personal.

Limp Wrist

This is a handshake common to and from women for many years, and as women and their rights have evolved, many women now will see this as an insult. This is not an entire handshake but is usually more characteristic of a "finger shake."

Good Shake

A good shake is firmly held, three shakes at maximum, while maintaining eye contact. Remember that signals and signs are a matter of perception and may not always seem as they appear. In order to make an accurate assessment of someone's body language, you must also take into account the words and expressions that are being used.

CRITICISM HURTS ME SO DEEPLY

We have spent our entire lives listening to some form of criticism. As children, we were criticized for behavioral issues; as adults, we may be criticized in relationships or in the workplace. While many people do not object to criticism as long as it is constructive, others languish at the thought of their actions being any less than perfect. If you are the vocal or aggressive parent, then you may have a better understanding of how deeply criticism can hurt. While criticism can make you feel guilty and worthless, if mishandled, it can also cause anger. As you know from previous chapters, anger is a way for parents who are traumatized by the birth experience to release their feelings, to cover the pain from the trauma of the birth experience.

In order to handle the criticism befittingly, you must first evaluate the criticism. Take what is important, put it aside, and disregard the rest. In order to evaluate what is important, you must gather as much information as you possibly can. You may ask, when you already feel inept and then are criticized for your actions, why you would want to ask anyone to clarify his criticism. You would rather forget you ever heard it. While this may be true, you might actually gain more positive feedback by requesting more information. If a nurse tells you that it is better not to hold the baby a certain way, you have two choices: you can not hold the baby that way and shrink away in embarrassment because you did it wrong, or you can ask for further instruction. What would be a better way to handle the baby? Turn the criticism into an instrument for learning.

I WANT A SECOND OPINION

As medical advances have been made, the cost of malpractice insurance has skyrocketed, as has the number of lawsuits. More and more doctors are encouraging second opinions. You may find that unusual or wonder to yourself, are they not confident enough in their own decisions that they need to seek outside affirmation? This is not necessarily true. Medicine is a science, and there are no black and white answers. There are, however, plenty of areas that are subject to interpretation. Since each baby is so unique and has such a distinct set of medical problems, each one requires a treatment plan like no other. Each baby may also respond differently to the same or similar approaches.

If a medical provider does not suggest a second opinion, do not think that he will take offense if you do. You may also find that you prefer a doctor who specializes in your baby's condition to evaluate and determine a course of treatment. Keep in mind that in most NICUs, while the neonatologist is the primary care physician for your baby, he consults other physicians, including those that specialize in matters of the heart, lungs, gastrointestinal system, and many other areas. You can ask your doctor for a referral; your baby's doctor may feel more comfortable with an opinion that comes from a colleague, which they can accurately assess, rather than from a stranger.

There can be a host of other reasons to seek a second opinion, including insurance, religious beliefs, or the exploration of alternative treatments. Seeking a second opinion is not right for everyone. If you are comfortable with the information that is being given to you and are confident in your provider's abilities, you may not wish to cloud the path with other opinions.

Chapter 9

Views from Others
in the Baby's Life

EMPATHY WITH A DOSE OF REALITY

By Dr. Juan Carlos Roig, FAAP

Because of present-day conditions in medicine, the number of premature deliveries worldwide is rising alarmingly. Nowadays, parents may encounter difficulty in obtaining prenatal care or, what can be far worse, choose not to seek it. Also alarming is that primary care physicians in many areas of the United States are having increasing difficulty in obtaining subspecialty consults for their most delicate cases. A significant increase in the number of cesarean sections and premature deliveries is occurring. The number of some medical subspecialties and of practicing obstetricians is declining daily. This effect may be due, in part, to existing medicolegal conditions today in our country.

These conditions may be predisposing a growing number of parents to become unexpectedly familiar with an area in some regional medical centers known as the NICU, or the neonatal intensive care unit. For many parents, having an infant in the NICU may be a repeat experience. For most it will be entirely new. Regardless of which group one belongs to, it is usually a very difficult experience.

The most basic observation that can be made and shared in common between all who will spend any amount of time in the NICU is that while visiting, they will encounter no healthy babies or parents that are happy being there.

Generally, a premature infant is defined as any infant delivered at or prior to 37 weeks of gestation. The accepted standard term is

40 weeks. The premature infants will all be exposed to the world outside their mothers' wombs sooner than the period that nature intended for their safe maturation, having to survive without their mothers' help from then on. This new setting is full of high-tech machines and equipment designed to perform the function of replacing the mother's uterus. Nothing exists today that can replace the mother's uterus as a substitute for the proper maturation of an infant. For lack of a better substitute our technology is only second-best. Modern science does not have the ability to replace these infants in the mother once delivered.

Under ideal conditions, all infants need months of development and maturation in the safety of their mothers' wombs. What should anyone expect regarding the outcome for these infants if delivered often as early as 15 or 16 weeks before their due dates? Some of these infants will be delivered weighing less than one pound.

Once delivered, the neonate will have to rely on the function of its vital organs for survival. The more premature, the less developed the infant's brains, heart, lungs, kidneys, bowel, and other organs. Can parents expect the infant to survive? If so, can they realistically expect him to do so free of complications? The answer is yes, but not always. When considering the smallest or sickest, each new day's existence represents a monumental feat that must be accomplished with our support in order to survive.

Owing to regionalization of the centers providing the higher or more subspecialized level of care required for these patients, parents will often have to travel a distance to deliver or may be transferred to a different center prior to delivery of their infant. More and more frequently, these transfers will lead to a particularly difficult situation, where the medical team ultimately involved in the care of these infants will not have the time to discuss or prepare the parents for what to expect. This situation is particularly difficult for both parties involved and is presently occurring with more frequency. Although no ideal condition exists for any parent having what will be a sick newborn, it would certainly be less stressful for everyone involved if some anticipatory guidance were to take place prior to delivery.

Often due to the sensationalistic nature of today's media or to anecdotal reports, some parents will have preconceived expectations regarding the medical outcome of their infant. These expectations can be very unrealistic. When unable to speak with these parents prior to the delivery of the infant, the caregivers will not be able to prepare them for what to expect. Quite often, what parents expect and what they are first told by the caregivers can be drastically different.

It is very important to mention that with rare exceptions, everyone that is part of the care team of providers (physicians, nurses, respiratory therapists, etc.) will always try to convey a bedside message of optimism. Because of the legal requirements that exist, today's practice requires this message to be brutally honest and based on statistical figures and medical facts. When applicable, the caretakers are required to delineate every possible complication associated with as well as all possible morbidity related to a particular infant's condition, regardless of how remote it may be. Simply stated, parents will frequently receive a very grim overview as part of the introductory exchange that will take place after admission. Invariably, this negative preface will very often define the relationship that will result between the parents and the NICU care team. Regardless of their background and even prior experiences, all the parents will experience anxiety, feelings of guilt, and distrust during their time spent in the NICU.

It is essential for parents to understand the following: Just like in any other highly specialized area of work, the people who work in the NICU understand the importance of completing a common mission—to achieve and to maintain the well-being of every patient who comes there. To these caretakers, the NICU is more than just a job. Although many of the people who work in NICUs have had a relative or known a friend who at some time or another had an infant there, no one would want to trade places with a parent of a sick neonate interned there. We can only begin to imagine and empathize with these parents and how they must feel during this time. It is impossible for anyone other than these parents to comprehend this hardship, and it is even more difficult to endure it. It is very important, however, to realize that we are all human, even the caretakers. As such, all involved will have different personalities, dispositions, and so on. Coupled with the anxiety and stress of having a sick child in the NICU, these differences can lead to interactions between caregivers and parents that may be uncomfortable.

Another important fact is that as parents, we are all innately programmed to protect our children from the time they are born. Everyone that becomes a parent assumes the role with some control over his actions and is used to intervening accordingly. However, when parents give birth to a sick infant, they will have to relinquish most of their control over the ensuing care. This is particularly difficult for most parents. During this time, mutual trust between the parties involved is essential. Achieving this trust today is more difficult because of the preconceived opinions the general public has about hospitals and all caretakers. Invariably, this situation leads to apprehension and suspicion about those who will have so much to say over the life of the infant.

The experience of many of the NICU caregivers is that there is a growing number of parents who, when facing this shift in control, begin to load themselves with clinical information. This is usually done via the Internet. This behavior may progress to become an obsession. What may so often begin as just a comfort measure often turns excessive, causing these parents to abandon the role of parents to the sick infant and become untrained "doctors." This change can have negative effects on the very essential parent-doctor relationship. It can be a monumental task for parents to assimilate what may be very large amounts of clinical data, to process it and understand its application to their sick infant. What parents must always remember is to ask questions frequently. Some independent research is encouraged and can even be therapeutic. However, if any topic contained therein appears confusing or different, one should be prompt to seek guidance whenever possible.

In most instances the predisposing event that may lead to a premature or a sick newborn delivery may be preventable. In the specific case of a preeminent premature delivery, early intervention and preventive medicine is priceless. In the realm of the premature infant, size does matter. Generally, those infants who weigh more tend to have better outcomes. Since each day any infant remains in its mother's womb may represent an increase in fetal size, those mothers who have cared to seek and set up prenatal care are more likely to have a better outcome for their infants. A good relationship between the parents and their obstetrical or perinatal care provider is of extreme importance. In today's managed health care environment, and because of the effects personal injury lawyers have had on medicine, subspecialists are becoming harder to find.

If delivered, these premature infants will need to survive disconnected from the inimitable environment that was their mothers' uterus and placenta. In order to survive, the premature infant will need to depend on the function and efficiency of their underdeveloped organs. Present-day technology is able to augment and support the functions of some of the organs vital for survival. It cannot, however, replace their functions. This means that it becomes necessary for the infant's own organs to function at least to a degree where the infant can survive. When the basic development of these organs has not yet taken place, the infant will likely expire. In those cases the caretakers only succeed in prolonging this period, with the inevitable outcome occurring later. If enough development of the vital organs (brain, lungs, heart, kidneys) has already taken place by the time in which the interruption takes place and the infant is delivered, he may survive. Currently, this gestational age is 24 weeks plus or minus 1 week. Frequently, the time of hospitalization needed for these infants to achieve the appropriate size and capabilities needed for discharge is often the balance to reach the 40 weeks of a full-term gestation. During that time in the NICU those infants who are the smallest will most often have the most complicated clinical courses. When one considers how immature these infants can be at birth, their survival can truly be considered miraculous. During their stay in the NICU the infants' courses can be so full of clinical fluctuations that parents often compare them to riding a roller coaster. Even with the most strict of safety conditions in place, the NICU environment these infants are born into are mostly just noisy, bright, nonsterile, and extreme in nature. It is truly amazing how these very sick infants can manage to adapt to the drastic conditions they are made to face.

During this journey in the NICU the hardest role to assume will be that of being parent. Ideally, whether by design or not, parents should be part of the care team. The more mutually respectful, efficient, and friendly this relationship becomes, the better the experience and the outcome are likely to be. All parties involved should endeavor to overcome personal differences for the good of the infant patient. Harmony is of vital importance, as is mutual respect. Both parents should expect to be involved in the process. The degree of involvement can vary depending on personal tolerance. The daily information regarding the infant's status and plan of care can be confusing to some. When something about the care of your infant does not make sense, a parent should not be afraid to ask. Information can be obtained in many ways. Generally, the care team will update parents at the bedside after work rounds have taken place. If this does not take effect, a parent can and should ask for a meeting with either the doctor or the nurse practitioner when mutually possible, or even for a simple phone call. Sometimes even well-intentioned practitioners can have a difficult time making it to the prearranged meeting because of the nature of the NICU (the sick and dying will require the most immediate attention). A parent, however, should never feel that it is an imposition to ask for information regarding the status of their sick infant.

Without doubt, the most readily available and most important resource for any parent during the NICU stay is the bedside nurse. Most units will have one neonatologist per 24-hour shift. The assignment of nurses to patients is generally smaller. The nurse is the single most important person bridging the gap between doctors and the parents. In many instances the NICU nurses act much like surrogate parents to the infants. They are very protective and watch over them as they would a family member. Again, managed care has also had an impact on nursing assignments.

It is generally more difficult for anyone, even trained persons, to deliver bad news about an infant to the family. Unfortunately, on arrival to the NICU, most infants are critically ill. Certainly because so many persons can be involved in the care of these infants, there may be a myriad of different personalities, cultural and ethnic backgrounds, that the parents will become exposed to. The resultant rapport may vary. In no way should these occurrences affect the goal and clinical plans of the care team toward any infant. These situations may require an increase in mutual effort from both parties in order to maximize the communication necessary to achieve the highest degree of trust and best outcome.

The best care for any patient is always easier to achieve once good rapport and mutual trust are established. Just as it is important for a doctor or nurse to tell parents when they do not know the answer to a question or clinical situation, it is also important for a parent to understand this. No one should be offended by a request for a second opinion about an infant's status. More often, a caretaker's initial impressions are validated through this process. Once again, because of managed care, this can prove to be difficult to obtain.

The more harmonious the relationship between the parents and care team becomes, the easier it is to achieve the care plan goals set for a particular infant. As the infant becomes more stable and is able to perform the necessary tasks needed for his discharge (tolerate feeds, maintain body temperature, gain weight, etc.), the clinical emphasis will shift toward enabling the parents to assume the role of primary caretaker. The training may involve the learning of complicated procedures, such as administration of drugs, handling breathing apparatuses, and using feeding tubes, or may be relatively simple, such as performing routine feedings. Once again, the better the rapport that exists, the easier this process of passing the baton becomes.

The fact is that most infants in the NICU will survive to make it home to their families. The sooner parents seek and obtain adequate prenatal care, the better the outcome for their infant generally becomes. Once delivered and in the NICU, the time there for many infants is the equivalent of a marathon race. During this time, parents are expected to visit and marginally partake initially and to gradually become more immersed in the care as the infant becomes more stable. During the hospital course, everyone may experience a wide range of emotional states. Among these could be anxiety, self-doubt, depression, anger, joy, and countless other emotions. Despite the flaws existing in health care today as well as the imperfections innate to any particular NICU, the goal of care for these infants should always remain the same: to provide these infants with the most advanced and most dignified level of care available. This should be achieved, despite personal differences or the cultural or economic status of an infant. Everyone involved should strive to achieve the best care available for the common good of these very sick infants.

WORDS OF WISDOM FROM THE DOCTOR
By Debra Anne Jones, MD, FACOG

Women walk into my office every day overwhelmed by the thought of having a new baby. The excitement and joy generated within the woman and her family during that single moment when they realize that a perfect life will enter the world is one life's most profound experiences. The hopes and dreams for the life they have created are endless. I am an obstetrician and maternal fetal medicine specialist. As maternal fetal specialist, I have specialized training in the care and treatment of complicated pregnancies. I work together with obstetricians to provide an evaluation of a high-risk pregnancy and structure a treatment plan on the best medical evidence available.

I have the unfortunate task of sometimes having to shatter those dreams when the unexpected occurs. While as doctors, we do our best to give you the most realistic outcomes based on medical science and experience, we also make every effort to continue to instill hope. At that very moment, so many women feel that their worlds are crumbling. Even when they suspected problems with the pregnancy, hearing a diagnosis other than "everything is fine" is devastating. It is not uncommon for women to be unprepared as to what to ask or what to do. As doctors, with families of our own, we understand initial reactions of fear and encourage you and your family to digest the information and schedule further follow-up for questions and concerns. Understanding that your maternal fetal medicine specialist cannot always guarantee a good outcome or may not be able to give solid answers to your questions is sometimes frustrating. Realize that medicine is a science with limitations.

I have found that one of the most difficult aspects of my job is not being able to give guarantees but still asking that you trust me with ensuring that you and your baby receive the best possible medical care. The process can be challenging. However, it is the trust that is essential in developing a cooperative relationship between you and your physician. It is the cornerstone to the best outcome for the pregnancy.

We are in the information era, and patients want all the information that they can get. It is commonplace for patients to reach out to the Internet and equally as common for them to trust the information they retrieve. My opinion on the Internet as it relates to your pregnancy is that the Internet is a source of information, but it can also be your enemy. All information is not created equal. The source of the information is as important as the knowledge itself. The safest places to acquire information are Web sites or agencies that are nationally and internationally recognized. These include societies, journals, and books. A word of caution: If you have limited medical background, use the patient-friendly area of the Web site in analyzing medical studies. Medical studies are difficult even for the most seasoned professional. If you feel compelled to obtain a more in-depth understanding of a subject, make sure you take into account all factors, such as secondary diagnoses or conditions. Remember that it is also important to know when the study was done. The importance of the study in the literature and the statistics used to analyze the data along with other factors may impact the results. More importantly, keep in mind that every patient is different. Just as with DNA, there are never two identical sets of circumstances. My advice is to use the information as background, but trust your physician to make the appropriate choices for your particular set of circumstances.

Communication is a powerful tool. Realizing that there is no single drug, test, or procedure that is the "cure" is critical. Your physician should use the best available medical evidence to guide your care. Challenge your maternal fetal medicine specialist to discuss your diagnosis treatment and possible outcome. The maternal fetal medicine specialist should give you a realistic picture without taking your hope. As with your obstetrician, if your maternal fetal medicine specialist is not willing to take the time to address your concerns, consider a second opinion or change specialists. If you feel that your questions have been answered and you need additional time to cover all of your concerns, your maternal fetal medicine specialist should provide you with all the time you need. Understand that your maternal fetal medicine specialist has other patients who are under the same stresses arising from unexpected, high-risk complications. Make sure your maternal fetal medicine specialist speaks your language and you understand all the information and steps to ensure that you are doing what is best for your and your baby's health. I have always felt that as a provider, it is more than a job of just hearing your concerns; it is really listening and trying to understand your concerns and feelings. As the mother carrying the child, you have the most insight into how your body and baby are behaving on a 24-hour basis.

These good communication skills with your maternal fetal medicine specialist will help you to deal with feelings such as loss of control, hopelessness, anger, fear, guilt, and depression. Knowledge will also empower you as a parent and will help you understand the limitations of medicine and give you realistic expectations as to what to expect at delivery and in the future. The road of a premature infant can sometimes be very long.

While it is unrealistic to think that as doctors, we have the ability to be available at all times to all patients, it is not unrealistic that you have someone available to assist you along the way. This is where the perinatal nurses can become an invaluable tool to you and your family.

Perinatal nurses work in conjunction with your obstetrician and maternal fetal medicine specialist to provide comprehensive care from the time you are diagnosed with a high-risk pregnancy until delivery. Perinatal nurses are trained to teach parents and their families how to best deal with their diagnosis. They are trained to provide emotional support for the patient and answer general questions. You should feel free to ask your perinatal nurse questions regarding your care, both in the inpatient and outpatient settings. Many times, they have practical solutions to many of the challenges that you and your family are facing, from tips on bed rest to helping you to recognize contractions and fetal activity. Develop a connection with your nurse; she is much more available to you on a daily basis than the maternal fetal medicine specialist will be. If your questions involve medical problems or issues that need to be addressed to the maternal fetal specialist, the nurse will ensure that the questions are answered. Your nurses are your connection to the physician.

Another common figure in the birth of preterm infant is a neonatologist. A neonatologist is a pediatrician with special training in caring for newborns who are sick and require intensive specialized care after birth. Many times, your first visit with him is when time seems to be standing still. You are still unaware of all the information concerning your diagnosis and what to expect. No one is ever fully ready for his first visit with the neonatologist. With all the knowledge and support you have acquired on your journey to prepare yourself for this challenge, this is still a time of uncertainty. To better prepare yourself, ask your ob/gyn or maternal fetal medicine specialist to outline what to expect at the time of your baby's birth.

Another suggestion I regularly make to my patients is that if available, meet with your NICU to best discover what to expect in the upcoming days, weeks, or even months. They can best guide you through the maze and help develop a trusting relationship with the

NICU team. The team will more than likely be present during your delivery as a safety measure for the baby. By knowing who they are and what to expect when you first enter the NICU, you can relieve some of the stress of the unknown. The NICU can be a very overwhelming place when you are not accustomed to a hospital setting.

Most doctors who practice in the field of obstetrics not only do it for the love of medicine, but also because of the joy that we receive in bringing life into this world and starting so many new families for so many different people. Our goal as doctors is to provide the patient the best possible emotional and medical support available in the least stressful manner. The best overall advice I can offer to you as you go through this challenging time in your life is to understand that life and medicine are unpredictable: Expect the unexpected, and hope for the best.

> No matter how deep your sorrow you are not alone. Others have been there and will help share your load if you will let them. Do not deny them the opportunity.
>
> —*Amy Hilliard Jenson*

I AM AN NICU NURSE

By Eileen Penque

Working as a registered nurse in a level 3 neonatal intensive care unit is rewarding and challenging. Each day that I walk into the NICU, I feel proud to be part of an outstanding group of health care providers. I have worked as a nurse for 22 years at the same hospital, 19 of those years in the NICU. I have watched thousands of babies pass through the doors, and thanks to a joint effort of the medical providers and families of these precious beings, we see more and more happy endings.

Over the years, I have witnessed significant advances in the care of preemies. This is evidenced by the improved survival rates of all preemies but especially those who are critically ill and micropreemies. Just as medicine has changed, so have the trends in society. I have seen an increasing number of women in their mid-thirties to forties having babies. Since this population is more likely to have premature infants, I have had a great deal of exposure to them.

Many of the nurses I work with have weathered the years as long as I have, and some have started and ended into retirement without ever leaving the NICU. Their love and dedication to patient care is overwhelming, and they are nothing short of being miracle workers. The NICU is full of miracles, and we must call them miracles because these babies sometimes will defy all the odds. Outsiders to the NICU see it as a place of sadness and grief. Even friends and family of nurses comment how heartbreaking it must be to work with such tragic cases. My reply is always the same: The joy in the NICU far exceeds the pain. While the roller coaster of emotions for the families seems, at times, unbearable, the end result, as we watch these babies leave to go to happy, loving homes, erases all the traumas.

In the NICU in which I am employed it is standard protocol to orientate families who are at risk for delivering preterm babies. Each mom, dad, or caregiver introduced to our unit is overcome by emotion and disbelief as he or she enters the unit and sees all the foreign machines and babies so small and frail that they hardly look human. This was not their plan for the perfect delivery or the perfect baby. It is often unexpected and hard to comprehend all that is presented to them. The anxiety, fear, and uncertainty of what is to come are emotions that we as nurses recognize, but we can only provide limited information as the baby has not yet arrived. We will never tell you how you should be feeling, nor we will we ever dismiss your feelings.

I tell my families (I refer to them as my families because I feel a strong connection to their pain) that there will be steps forward and steps backward. I also recognize the tremendous responsibility and faith that they must have in me to make it through such a difficult ordeal. I feel that just as important as my medical knowledge and ability to care for the baby is their participation in the baby's care. From the very beginning I want my families to be part of a team effort in the care of their baby. In order to become part of our team, they must be familiar with all the members of the neonatal team. This includes your baby's doctors, nurse practitioners, nurses, respiratory therapists, discharge planner, developmental therapists, and a host of other practitioners who will come and go during your stay.

Not all health care providers have the bedside manner that we as nurses have, partly because they have less interaction with the parents and baby. However, I encourage parents to make time to speak to the neonatologist or nurse practitioner about their baby's condition. They need to put a face with a name. Aside from the nurse, these practitioners will be the most common in the daily care of your baby.

The first time that parents see their baby, all the NICU equipment that is connected to the baby can be overwhelming. Many parents appear to be in a fog or state of shock. Over time, as reality sets in, families become better adjusted as they learn what each machine is and its function. I think it is important to be honest with your families. It is my goal to promote a bonding relationship between parent and baby. I want each and every parent to feel confident in his ability to care for this baby. He will be walking out the door with this baby. A baby will sense a less than confident parent. I will teach you how to touch the baby and soothe the baby. I encourage families to ask questions, and I will keep them informed of the baby's progress or setbacks. I will never be anything but honest with a parent. This helps families to face the realities but also to become positive, confident caregivers for their baby. I take extra steps to acknowledge my parents' presence at their baby's bedside, update them, and answer any questions not once, but every time I see them.

Dealing with some parents can be challenging. The parents usually fall into one of three categories. There are the self-sufficient, confident parents who jump right in. These parents love to be taught, and when they visit their baby, they are independent, able to handle the baby and provide care, such as temperature readings, diaper changes, and feeding. Then there are the needy, emotional parents who need a lot of TLC and have a hard time functioning when it comes to any type of hands-on care of their baby. They are usually still in shock, and the situation seems surreal to them. They are scared and fearful when the nurse must leave their bedside in order to take care of another baby. Sadly, there are also those parents who rarely call or visit for whatever reasons, and there are always excuses. Some of these parents are too afraid to face reality, and others just feel that the baby is better off without them. The reasons are endless on both sides of the spectrum, but a baby without parents can slow the healing process of the baby.

Most of the babies at our hospital are patients for about one to two months, depending on age and course of treatment. During this time the parents and the nurses will experience a number of emotions. Caregivers as well as parents have good and bad days. Maybe a nurse may be preoccupied with problems in his personal life. Just as parents sometime feel overwhelmed, so can a nurse. Owing to rules set by others higher than ourselves, our patient loads may be heavy, or we may have one baby that requires extra attention, and paperwork is always an issue. It would be nice if each baby could have his own nurse, but in the world of modern medicine, that is not a reality. A shortage of nurses and hospital funding makes overworked nurses a common occurrence in most hospitals. I think our dedication to the babies would not allow us to do anything but the best that we can. Some parents understand this, and others do not. I think our NICU provides the best care in our particular area.

Everyone's NICU experience will be different, as with everything in life. One of the most critical aspects of your baby's care will be to form an open line of communication with the health care providers. This is secondary to bonding with your baby by visiting your baby as much as possible. Get to know your baby and feel comfortable with his daily care. This includes holding, proper positioning, bottle or breast feeding, changing diapers, bathing, and taking your baby's temperature. Do not be afraid to ask questions; that is the only way to get answers. Your baby is different from a full-term baby, and while instinct may kick in for most of your baby's needs, you have to keep in mind that his medical needs are a priority.

While we recognize that the NICU is no place like home, the only home your baby has ever known is your womb, so your familiar touch and smell will feel like home to the baby. We also encourage reading a story at the bedside or playing a taped recording of your voice, hanging family pictures, or bringing baby clothes and blankets or a personal object, such as a small stuffed animal. As nurses, we understand that parents cannot visit every day. This does not mean we think that you are a bad parent. Parents need their rest so that they can take care of their baby, and they need to know that it is okay. While we may not always agree with decisions that you make, we are not there to judge. Every baby and parent in our unit is different, as are the nurses. We are all from different backgrounds, have different thoughts and ideas and unique personalities. We also all have different reasons for wanting to be in the NICU.

We recognize that these personality differences and the emotions that you are experiencing can sometimes create conflict. Let us face it: You are not going to have a good day every day. Everyone's emotions and personalities are different, and some just clash. Some parents feel helpless when unable to care for their baby or if the baby has a setback. Parents can express those emotions in a number of different ways, not always positive. Since we are only human, some of us will take it well, while others will not. Even if we do take something to heart, we recognize that your reactions are to the trauma you are experiencing and not to us personally.

We do not get offended if a parent prefers that only certain nurses care for their baby or that certain ones do not. Just as a parent may have a favorite nurse, we also sometimes have favorite patients or families. Some nurses enjoy parent teaching, and others may be more concerned with patient comforting. While some nurses are hands-on care superior, they may not enjoy parent interaction. Every caregiver has strengths and weaknesses, and this could influence a parent's opinion of him. Our personal feelings toward the family are in no way indicative of how we care for your baby. Your baby will always receive the utmost professional care. When a parent becomes verbally abusive and demanding or simply has a highly charged, emotional personality, we will make every attempt to understand that the underlying emotions are related to fear of what is happening to her baby. However, there comes a point where a line needs to be drawn if the behaviors are disruptive to the care of the baby.

Probably the most difficult thing as a nurse to see as a preemie is progressing in the NICU is a setback. Parents must be reminded that premature babies may develop infections or have developmental delays and that some setbacks may require surgery or delays because of disease. While this may be the normal course of a developing preemie, the impact on the nurses is equally as great as on the parents. Some parents find it extremely difficult to focus during times of crisis, and we hope that relationships that have developed with the team assist in comforting the parents. Better to be comforted by a friend than by a stranger. However, we also recognize that we are the easiest targets for blame. Parents blame doctors, nurses, therapists—anyone they can—because their child may not be perfect. While we are not perfect, and we do make mistakes—we are only human—every precaution is taken in the NICU to check and double-check to ensure that your baby is receiving the best possible care.

What some parents fail to understand is how deep the connection is to these babies, so frail and gentle. Most of us in the NICU are not there just because we want to be medical providers; we are there because we believe that these babies are the most precious of God's creatures and deserve every fighting chance to survive and grow to be something special. We care for these babies day after day, and while shifts change and rotations change, our feelings do not. We more than likely have the same babies on more than one occasion, and if we do not, we know about what is going on. Our lunches, breaks, celebrations, and defeats all rotate around these babies. When we walk into the NICU, we are walking into our homes. Most of us spend more waking hours with the babies of the NICU than we do with our own children. Our own feelings become mixed as we watch the babies walk out the door. We feel joy of the success and sadness of the parting. We only hope that parents will keep us reminded of the gift they received through pictures. We hold reunions not for the parents, but for us to see the children they have become.

If it was a perfect world, no one would be born premature. But it is not, and thankfully, there are extremely talented caregivers to provide your child with a very significant chance for survival. While some of theses infants are taken to be angels, the odds of survival are greater and increasing every day with modern medical technology. When we do lose a baby, the pain is felt by all. The tears are as real as they would be for someone in our own families. Luckily for us, most often, they are tears of joy, knowing that another family has survived the emotional journey of parenting a baby in the NICU.

FROM PROFESSIONAL TO PATIENT

By Emily Piper

I sat in the hospital bed, down the hall from my office. I worked as a psychologist at a children's and women's health center. This time, however, I was not sitting with a patient. Ironically, I was the patient. I explained to the therapist sitting beside me that I had thought of pregnancy as being fairly straightforward. I questioned how this could be happening to me. I ate well, I went to prenatal classes, I never touched a drop of alcohol. I came from "a long line of breeders" (my mother's words). This was not supposed to happen! I told my assigned therapist, with some obvious shame, that I had walked by the NICU about twice a day for six years, to and from my office and the hospital cafeteria, and never once stopped in, never once took a moment to think about what went on inside.

In my heart of hearts I abruptly recognized that I was about to be introduced to the world of the NICU. I suppose that this is what talking to a therapist does: It brings clarity, even if through excruciating pain. This is what I supposedly learned all those years ago in grad school and even during my own analysis. I realized, however, that I had spoken to my analyst from the clichéd perspective of the "worried well" or the "classic neurotic." This situation was completely different. I now spoke from an intensely raw and primitive place. I was not talking to this therapist about my grades, my latest weekend romance, or whether or not I was becoming my mother . . . I was talking about my baby and whether or not she would survive.

Although I had counseled so many families about their sick children, I had never anticipated the terror, exhaustion, and confusion that came with their experiences. Intellectually, I "knew" what they were feeling simply because they told me. Wow. What a blow to my ego, as it was only then—sitting in that awful bed, with the very kind and truly compassionate therapist—that I truly knew what terror, exhaustion, and confusion really were. Similarly, I knew how off the mark I had been all those years. I knew how distant I had been from my patients, although I could not fault myself. Life was not an ivory tower.

Six hours later, my daughter was born by cesarean section at 25 weeks' gestation, weighing one pound three ounces. Soon after, I was wheeled into the NICU for the first time. I quickly learned that as much as I wanted to maintain my professional identity with the neonatal team, it would be impossible. I had to surrender and become completely immersed in parenthood if I wanted to maintain any form or anonymity and be true to the humanity that I was currently living. Nevertheless, what I learned was that an experience so personal and private as the birth of a daughter seemed very public.

Being a patient in my own hospital, my own workplace, and surrounded by familiar health care professionals who I had gone to coffee with—at some point in time . . . maybe three weeks ago?—was compounded by the exposure I felt in a room with 39 other babies. I was 1 family in a room of 40—in an expansive openness with the relentless ringing of beeps and buzzes—every baby's story felt completely open, as the babies did lay "open" in their tiny incubators. I felt so vulnerable. I thought, this is what parents talk about when their child is in the hospital. I am living their once described nightmare, but just slightly different, as this nightmare was my own.

I soon experienced firsthand the miscommunication between team players, the hundreds of staff members, and the question of continuity of care. Comparatively, I experienced what it was like to really bond with a special nurse and to trust certain professionals on the team. I learned how the NICU staffers could help my daughter, if I let them, if I let go of my professional, clinical, and defensive approach, if I truly allowed myself to experience the ignorance of being a first-time parent—even under such uniquely stressful circumstances.

I learned what it was like to have the urge to read my daughter's chart, even though I knew I would not be able to read half the medical scratch, a short hand for an already complex jargon. Truly, I just wanted to see if they had written anything about my daughter's "neurotic mother." I learned about that urge—an urge I had questioned so many times in the past. How selfish of me, really. I learned what it meant to "advocate for your child" with an empty, robotic tone . . . I now know a more accurate recommendation would be to "love your child, no matter what." I learned what it was like to be on "the other side"—what it was like to be a patient. I learned what it was like to let go of the process of intellectualization and embrace the experience, no matter how painful or challenging it was.

Most importantly, I learned that emotional depth is not something that can be learned in a textbook. It is something that life provides, with all of its edginess and imperfections. I wholeheartedly thank my daughter for all of this. She has succeeded in putting me in my place—a humbling but necessary experience.

Chapter 10

Self-Empowerment

"I feel so vulnerable, so exposed. I am in a unit with so many other babies, and everyone knows everything about my baby, except me. I don't understand the lingo or the medical scribble on the charts which hang on my baby's isolette." How do you keep your self-confidence, your self-esteem, and continue to feel worthy when you feel so ineffective as a parent and a caretaker? There are so many times in the NICU when you will feel that it is pointless to stand by your baby's bed. It is as if you have been placed next to your baby for the sole purpose of the viewing pleasure of those who walk through the NICU door. You feel as though there is nothing that you can do but hope for the best and fear the worst. As with so many of the other emotions discussed in this book, you must set realistic expectations of what will happen with the baby's medical condition and also what is in store for the baby's future.

So many women fear showing their vulnerability; it somehow in our minds correlates to weakness. You cannot develop full self-empowerment until you have accepted that you are in a vulnerable position. Exposing your vulnerability will actually open lines of communication for you. If you expose your vulnerability, you are actually breaking a cycle of trust and mistrust. You have to be careful not to be defensive but to accept truthfulness and compassion, which is what every member of the NICU is trying to express in his own special way.

KNOWLEDGE

Knowledge is a key step in giving yourself a sense of empowerment and becoming a part of the team of the NICU. There are thousands of resources available to you through the Internet, organizations, and other forms of media. Take the time to review them. For your perusal, there are a number resources listed in appendix C of this book. The more knowledge you have about your baby's medical condition, the more confident you will feel in discussing your baby's condition with medical providers and others. Your baby may have a number of medical issues, as most preemies do. Take each issue independently of the others and examine the subject related to it, the medications that are used, the forms of treatment, and the potential risks. Not only are you becoming an educated consumer, but you will be able to better advocate on your baby's behalf. While every baby is unique in the special care that he needs, no two hospitals will handle things in exactly the same manner. You may find that your hospital is the most up to date or that there are other procedures that you might have questions about.

OVERCOMING YOUR ANXIETIES

Managing your own emotions will also give you a sense of empowerment. Do not underestimate the power of emotions. Anxiety, guilt, anger, and depression can take hold of your mind, body, and spirit and cause you to react in ways that you never would under different circumstances. Once you have been able to master the skill of overcoming, or at minimum controlling, your emotions, you should feel a great sense of supremacy. We are all human and therefore subject to setbacks. Just as your baby will have medical setbacks, you will have emotional setbacks. Keep in the forefront of your mind that you have identified and tackled these emotions before and can confidently do it again. If anxiety is able to take control of your mind, you may come to regret your actions later. This is the most critical time in your baby's life, and you want to be as level-headed as possible.

REALIZE AND SUPERSEDE SELF-DEFEATING THOUGHTS

You feel like you cannot do anymore; you are emotionally and physically exhausted. You wonder how you can possibly continue on another day, week, or month.. The physical exhaustion is usually secondary to the emotional exhaustion that you feel in parenting a preemie. When the emotional and physical exhaustion comingle, you begin to have self-defeating thoughts. A negative and self-defeating thought pattern will make it difficult for you to continue on your journey of caring for your baby. These automatic self-doubting thoughts usually occur after a setback. The setback may be tension in the home from being away for an extended period of time, a medical setback, or another personal issue that causes you to think in a negative way.

Some of us find ourselves in the should-must-ought stage, where we apply this statement to every aspect of our lives: I should be able to handle this. I must stay at the hospital, and I ought to have known more about my baby's conditions. These are just examples of the thoughts that race through your head without any real time to think about what they really mean. Once you let the automatic negative thoughts begin, you will be bombarded with a series of irrational fears, which will cause anxiety. Try filling in the blanks and see what you think about yourself as it relates to how you are handling the experience.

I should be _____.
I must _____.
I ought to be _____.

Look back at these statements and review them carefully. Are you holding yourself to an impossible standard of perfection? Are these statements true, and based on what source are you sure they are true? Who said you should be able to handle the situation? Who said you must stay at the hospital? Who says that you ought to have known? In most cases you will find that the source setting the standard of how you should be feeling or what you should be doing is yourself. You are setting yourself up for failure by being overdemanding of yourself physically and emotionally.

WHAT A WONDERFUL PLACE

This theory is commonly referred to as guided imagery. Guided imagery is a therapeutic technique that is used to promote relaxation and healing through guided imagery. This tool can be used in a number of different areas as you experience the emotional roller coaster of parenting a preemie. However, we felt that it was especially useful in this chapter as the imagery is meant to empower and relax you, which will help in alleviating some of the ongoing experiences that you encounter as you travel the road of parenting a preemie. Guided imagery is a rather simple technique, and the key to making it work is to find that special place that is significant to you. For some it may be relaxing by the beach; for another it may be skiing down a mountain. It is a place or activity that gives you an overall sense of well-being. Since the likelihood of you being able to escape to your special place is probably very slim at this moment, you must recreate this place in your mind. Use the following steps in setting up the image in your mind.

1. Find a relaxing, quiet place to begin: a favorite chair, a comfortable bed.
2. Close your eyes and take deep, soothing breaths. You are releasing all the negative images from your mind and releasing all the tension that has built up in your muscles.
3. Now, with your eyes closed and your body relaxed, go to the special place. You should immediately start to have images of the place.
4. Focus on it more than just visually; focus on the colors, the shapes, the smells, and the sounds.
5. Allow yourself to become totally immersed in the experience.

You will find that the experience will relax you, if you are able to recognize the cues that guided imagery have allowed you in being able to relax. You can also recognize that negative images can create the opposite effect. If, when you are using guided imagery, you find that negative or intrusive thoughts are interfering, you must change those negative images to positive ones. Negative imagery can create anxiety equally as damaging as negative thoughts. If you feel that you cannot help yourself from the having these negative images, try the "knight-in-shining-armor" theory. Imagine yourself in the anxiety-arousing situation, but you are the one who is able to save the day and walk off into your special place together. Do not give up—there are a number of other recognized and accepted techniques. You just have to find the one that is appropriate for you.

JOURNALING

Journaling is another word for a diary: a very personal account of your thoughts, feelings, and expressions of emotion which you write as often as you desire. You can use a loose-leaf book or a fancy journal with a lock. What you express on the inside is what will count. Many women have found that journaling is an outlet for emotions but also a way to keep track of the baby's medical progress. You may find that as you journal your thoughts and feelings, you can refer back to the triumphs and setbacks to recognize internally how you were able to process those emotions and work through them. If you feel it necessary to track your baby's medical progress, this can be an invaluable tool as while you are a constant in the baby's life, a medical practitioner is not. Different shifts mean different doctors, and while the doctors and nurses take time to brief each other on the course and treatment of the baby, it cannot replace your valued input as you have been there every minute.

When it comes to your emotions, there is no right or wrong as to what you write. Your expressions are a way of self-healing—putting things into perspective so that you can move forward on the emotional journey. List out your anxieties, your fears, and the pain you feel. Set goals for yourself based on these negative feelings. While a support system is a necessary component in the healing process, it may not be enough. You may find that you have thoughts, fears, or dreams that you do not feel comfortable sharing. However, someday you may choose to share these with your baby or even your spouse.

Men especially have difficulty expressing their emotions in high anxiety–provoking situations. While they want to able to just fix everything, they cannot. They also feel helpless and, at times, maybe even shut out. Encourage all members of the family to share their thoughts and feelings. There may come a time when you can share them with each other. Resentment and hurt feelings that may have been overlooked during the highest periods of anxiety can manifest into problems in the relationship later.

RESTORING SELF-ESTEEM

In order to restore self-esteem, we must first know what it is. Self-esteem is the value that you place on yourself.

You value yourself as a person.
You take value in your achievements.
You are aware of how others see you.
You can identify your strengths.
You are able to recognize your weaknesses.
You have the ability to stand independently.

Low self-esteem is caused by attitudes or perceptions that your self worth is something less than that of others. Self-esteem is something that fluctuates on a daily basis and can be based on daily experiences. The creation of your self-esteem did not start with this experience in your life. Your self-esteem is something that has been cultivated over the years by your own thoughts, relationships, successes, and failures. Starting in childhood, your experiences led you to the level of self-esteem you have now. That level of self-esteem is going to have a direct impact on how you accept the triumphs and setbacks, how you involve yourself with the medical staff, and even how you parent your child once you go home.

Your baby may get a positive test result, and you feel as if you are floating on Cloud 9, or your baby may receive a negative result, and you feel as if your world has ended. Your self-esteem is affected by each and every event that enters into your life. The difference is that a person with high self-esteem is able to accept these challenges to his ego and bring something positive out of them. For the person with negative self-esteem, his inner voice is a harsh critic of himself that constantly criticizes and belittles his accomplishments. While parenting a premature infant is not the sole cause of low self-esteem, self-esteem problems can present themselves during this time to people for which they might otherwise not have been recognizable. Self-esteem can mask itself in people in a number of different ways.

The Faker

This person appears to be very happy on the outside but is really scared that someone might find out who he really is. He is absorbed with being considered a failure, and he uses the constant successes as a way to hide his own insecurities.

The Renegade

This person does not really care what people have to say about him or how people perceive him, unless they are important. Despite the appearance that he does not care, he takes criticism very much to heart and is constantly trying to prove his worth.

The Failure

This person acts like a failure, a constant whiner who says he cannot cope or cannot handle the challenges that are presented to him. This person is an underachiever and uses self-pity to get the attention of others.

While all three of these people, or any combination thereof, can create anxiety, they also can have a significant impact on relationships with family, friends, medical staff, and even, ultimately, the baby. There are a few important rules to remember in building your self-esteem and giving yourself the ultimate level of confidence that you are capable of.

Head Off What You Dread

The things that you believe are the worst are probably not as bad as they seem. Refer to controlling your worries, as discussed previously.

Forget about the Past

There may have been some ups and downs, and you may or may not have felt as if you failed at one time. Release those feelings. If at first you do not succeed, try again.

Talk It Out

The biggest mistake people make in communicating and interpreting each other is assumption. Assume nothing; identify your thoughts and feelings clearly so that you understand what other people are communicating to you and you to them.

We want you to develop a pattern of positive self-esteem. Positive self-esteem can create feelings of self-worth and value that will ultimately make you a happier person on the road to better relationships. Continued low self-esteem, on the other hand, can cause depression, unhappiness, insecurity, and poor confidence, personally and in your parenting ability.

So how do you get some of this positive self-esteem? If it could be bottled, what a happy world it would be. Self-esteem is something that does not come overnight; it takes time and nurturing, just as your preemie will. There are some positive actions you can take to cultivate positive self-esteem, starting with nurturing yourself.

Rest—Get a good night's sleep, eat in a healthy way, and exercise, even if it is just a walk around the hospital.
Good hygiene—Nothing makes us feel so good as to have a hot shower; a little makeup for women would not hurt either. Dress appropriately but comfortably.
Have some fun—Go to a movie, find a good book to read, or watch your soap operas during lunch.
Celebrate your triumphs—If you got a good evaluation at work or won a prize, you would celebrate. Celebrate everything, no matter how small: the gaining of a pound, being able to leave the baby without anxiety, and so on.

Finding ways to nurture yourself when you are not used to doing it can be difficult; if you have a hard time doing it, do it anyway. Fake it. When you treat yourself, even if you are faking it, slowly, you will come to believe that you can celebrate the successes. Whether the success is yours personally or the baby's, you must take credit for both as the baby would not have been able to be here were it not for your love and nurturing along the way.

A VIEW OF A POSITIVE, SELF-EMPOWERED PARENT

A positive, self-empowered parent is what we all strive to be. We want to be at our best and are so overwhelmed by the emotions associated with navigating this emotional journey that we become stuck in a rut at times or just have trouble moving to the next step. The following is a list of attributes associated with a positive, self-empowered parent:

☑ is able to manage and control emotions
☑ is able to manage and control interactions with others
☑ is able to be sensitive to the needs and views of others
☑ is able to recognize defensiveness in himself or others and manage the conflict appropriately
☑ is able to take pride in his accomplishments
☑ is able to recognize his imperfections and weaknesses
☑ is able to recognize that self-esteem is a core worth and not something that is going to be gained by some external stimulus.

Recognize that if you are able to check off even one item on this list, you are effectively on the road to self-empowerment. This list is by no means all inclusive, and as you grow as a person and parent, you will find your own definitions of self-esteem and confidence. As we discussed previously, this is just one part of the journey of parenting a preemie; you have the next 18 years to cultivate the remainder. Triumph in and celebrate each step you take. You cannot change the past, but you most certainly can influence the future.

Chapter 11

Anxiety and Focus on the Future

You have spent weeks, maybe months, focusing on strengthening your babies. You have addressed their every medical concern and done whatever is necessary to ensure that they have the best treatments available to them. Now you find yourself looking to the future, wondering how you can possibly make it through the next two to three years before finding out what the full effects of prematurity will be. You have convinced yourself that the toddler stage will be the magic age. Realistically, years down the road there may be lingering long-term effects that may present themselves. How can you relieve the anxiety and fears that you feel, so that they will not affect the development of your children? How can you focus on a future of the unknown?

In order to focus on the future it is necessary to have some starting point to guide you in the development of your child. The following is a list of areas that are commonly tracked in the performance of your baby as he is developing:

- **Physical**—This will be a physical assessment of your child's health, weight, height, hearing, and vision.
- **Cognitive**—This is a mental health term used to identify thinking, learning, and problem solving skills.
- **Gross Motor and Fine Motor Skills**—This is the quality of movement of the baby: how your baby moves, walks, grasps objects, and how coordinated your baby is.
- **Communication**—This assesses a baby's communicative skills, such as babbling, speech, language, and conversation skills.

- **Social/Emotional**—This is how your baby responds to others. The assessment measures how babies play independently and how they interact with others.
- **Adaptive Development**—This is an assessment of the need for assistance: can they feed, toilet, or dress themselves.

While you must rely on the medical professionals to provide you with the details and intricacies of each of the above categories, having a generalized understanding of what they are looking for in the development of your baby will help you to understand the process.

WHAT TO EXPECT IN DEVELOPMENT

As you leave the NICU you will have the opportunity to meet with a discharge planner/social worker or nurse depending on the hospital you are in. The person is tasked with giving you all the information you need to care for your baby and his specific needs. They will give you a wealth of information. They will also include standard follow up information with the developmental resource in your community. There is a federally funded program for children with disabilities that will use the information provided by your healthcare provider and their own in-depth evaluation in a number of developmental areas.

While it is expected that during the first two years of your baby's life, he will be behind in development as compared to a full-term baby, he will achieve the same developmental milestones, just at different ages. Your preemie's lag will catch up at approximately 2 years of age. You will always need to be alert in the future for subtle signs of learning disabilities from the age of 2 and beyond but anything of any serious consequence will have shown up by now. You can take comfort in knowing that the majority of preemies do not develop serious developmental disabilities. However, the sicker the newborn, the more likely it is that he will develop a delay or disability.

In looking at developmental delays it is important and encouraging to be able to adjust your child's age based on his prematurity. This is commonly referred to as the corrected age. For example if your child is 9 months and was born 3 months early, you will be looking for developmental stages of a 6 month old.

9 months chronological age
−3 months premature
=6 months corrected age.

Table 11.1
Developmental Milestones and What You Can Do to Help

Chronological Age of Baby	Developmental Activities	Reasons for Concern	Parenting Assistance
2–3 months	Can hold head upright, from parent's shoulder or when lying on stomach. Turns head from side to side from lying down position. May grasp objects in hand. Begins to respond to faces, most often to parents. Enjoys touching, soothing, cuddling. Smiles or coos. Kicks feet and hands. Startles at loud noises. Turns head toward bright colors, sound of voices, or shaking of a rattle.	Does not follow objects. Does not startle at loud sounds. Hands and feet seem very stiff or very loose. Baby seems overly sensitive to touch.	Hold, snuggle baby often. Sing to baby. Provide baby with different objects to grasp and hold. Expose baby to different textures and patterns. Imitate sounds of baby. Make eye contact. Use mobiles or an object that baby can attempt to reach for.
6 months	Able to roll over from stomach to back. Able to maintain good head control. Starts to reach and grab for objects. May be the beginnings of fear of strangers. Able to sit supported. Speaks more than two to three sounds. Able to laugh. Opens mouth for spoon.	Has difficulty lifting up from stomach. Not sitting, even with support. Not rolling over. Arches neck and back often. No effort to grasp toys or other objects. No response toward sound. No recognizable sounds, such as cooing. Not putting hands together or to mouth.	Allow baby to play with food and feel different textures. Initiate games that encourage touch and reflex, such as patty cake, drums, etc. Talk to baby often in complete sentences. Explain things to baby as you are doing them, e.g., making the bed, doing the dishes.
9 months	Sits up without any help. Able to throw a ball or other object. Imitates sounds or actions, clumsily. Understands a few words. Pulls self up to a standing position. Points index finger. Can take toys or other objects out of containers. Looks for hidden objects.	Difficulty grasping or picking up objects. Not able to sit up alone. Not imitating sounds. Not beginning to eat solid foods or self-feeding.	Encourage child to speak or vocalize sounds. Play hide and seek or other removal games. Ignore messes, pay attention to good behavior. Roll a ball to baby to encourage him to roll it back.

Chronological Age of Baby	Developmental Activities	Reasons for Concern	Parenting Assistance
12 months	May be able to walk with support. Begins to use two-syllable words: *mama, dada, baba.* Able to wave good-bye. Able to push buttons on toys or other objects. Enjoys looking at pictures or being read to. Able to follow instructions, such as "bring me" or "give a kiss." Drinks from a cup with help.	Not able to pick up finger foods. Does not search for objects that are hidden. Does not pay attention to books or other forms of visual stimulation for short periods. Prefers one side of the body to the other.	Read to child. Introduce child to picture books. Dance and play with infant. Set limits on undesirable behavior. Do not interrupt when you hear baby speaking. Encourage putting toys or other objects inside of other things. Encourage independent feeding.
18 months	Able to use crayons to scribble. Able to name things, such as people or objects. Pretend plays with toys or other objects. Walks up steps or runs. Builds objects with blocks or cups. Knows some body parts. Able to assist in getting dressed.	Not walking properly or on tiptoes. Difficulty using building blocks. Not using hands, still very oral with toys. Does not attempt to speak at 15–20 single words. Has difficulty following simple directions.	Read stories to child. Encourage sharing. Encourage block building. Encourage pretend play. Play games to identify body parts.
24 months	Able to kick a ball. Recognizes books, movies. Able to form three-word sentences. Able to jump or dance. Matches shapes. Able to vocalize needs, e.g., "bottle."	Not putting words together. Cannot identify basic pictures, e.g., cookie, bottle, baby. Lacks balance and coordination. Cannot follow simple instructions. Unable to vocalize needs or understand speech. Shows no interest in potty training.	Recite nursery rhymes and songs, leaving words out for child to fill in. Watch educational programming together. Read books. Encourage sharing and outdoor activities.

Chronological Age of Baby	Developmental Activities	Reasons for Concern	Parenting Assistance
36 months	Able to speak in small sentences.	Speech not understood.	Speak to and read to child regularly.
	Completes puzzles of three to four pieces.	Cannot copy or attempt a circle.	Encourage running and jumping.
	Balances on one foot.	Unable to understand commands, e.g., "in," "on," "up," "down."	Encourage sharing and playing with other children.
	Understands *big* and *little*.		
	Can sing songs and ask questions.		Use books, pictures, and imitation to show emotions.
	Recognizes feelings, e.g., sad, angry.	Cannot feed self without assistance.	

After the age of 2 years your child will be judged developmentally as if he was not premature. For the most up-to-date information on development of premature infants, see the resources included in this book. Generally speaking the following chart provides developmental milestones for preemies from the age of 2 months to 36 months.

BRINGING THE BABY HOME

You may have thought that all of the those feelings of anxiety and fear would disappear when the baby was released from the hospital. After all bringing your baby home has been your number one priority for so long. Not a day went by in the NICU when the thought did not cross your mind of how much longer would you have to endure an empty crib at home. How much longer until I will have a normal home with a happy, healthy baby?

As a parent and having experienced all the triumphs and setbacks in the NICU you have come to recognize that your baby is different, fragile, and susceptible to a host of germs and body-invading infections that a baby with a more developed immune system would be able to fight. Your fear, your concern, and your overheightened sensitivity to the baby's needs causes you anxiety. You have been trained in the NICU to scrub your hands and arms daily, wear masks when appropriate, and to keep everything that comes in contact with your baby sterile. You have known every step the medical professionals take in caring for your baby but for the most part have only been an onlooker.

Now as you head for home with your new baby, you not only have to face the normal stresses associated with bringing a new baby home but also with the medical issues surrounding your preemie. While you felt awkward and unfulfilled as a parent you are now concerned that you will not be able to fill the role that you have so desperately longed for. After you have brought your baby home and begin to settle in you may actually find that you miss the routines and the safety of the NICU. After all, if something were to go wrong with the baby the medical professionals were within screaming distance. The burden has now been placed on you to take care of the baby and watch for the signs and symptoms of medical problems arising. Although you feel immense joy in bringing your baby home, you still feel anxiety over your ability to parent this preemie and over the future role prematurity will play in your baby's life.

RECOGNIZING AND CONTROLLING YOUR ANXIETY

Research has shown that anxiety is the number one mental health problem among American women. A certain amount of anxiety is healthy. Anxiety can protect your baby from imminent harm and can motivate you to perform at top levels. When the anxiety causes dysfunction in your daily activities is when it is no longer healthy and you should seek professional help. There are a number of different types of anxiety; the most commonly experienced types of anxiety as they relate to parenting a preemie are generalized anxiety, posttraumatic stress disorder, panic, specific phobias, and obsessive compulsive disorder.

Generalized Anxiety

The theory behind generalized anxiety disorder is that you fear failure, fear that you will not be able to cope with the demands of the baby, fear the baby will die or again become seriously ill, or the fact that you have been under stress for such a long period of time already is causing you great anxiety. We believe that this is the most common form of anxiety experienced by women who have had a premature infant. If you are experiencing generalized anxiety as a result of the traumatic experience you might notice the following symptoms:

Snapping at People

Your body is full of all this extra energy and you may find that you have a short fuse. You may feel sorry or surprised at yourself for doing it but you just needed an outlet and someone had to be on the other end of it.

Increased Sensitivity

You have a heightened level of stress in your life, your hearing, smell, sight, touch, and smell are on high alert. Your body may feel edgy and ready to react to whatever threat arises to you or your baby.

Hypervigilance

Your body is on high alert; you will be able to notice new sounds, smells, or simply something out of place. Since you have a propensity to worry, you question the what or why to everything.

Overemphasized/Catastrophic Thinking

You take the smallest of concerns and exaggerate them to the extreme of a catastrophe. It cannot just be a cold, it must be pneumonia.

Cannot Sleep

This is probably one of the most difficult and common concerns for not only mothers of premature infants but new mothers in general. You cannot relax and therefore cannot sleep. You find yourself getting up in the night and checking to make sure that the baby is breathing or safe.

Difficulty Making Decisions/Choices

You worry over the consequences of the decisions or choices that you make. You are unable to accurately assess the impact of the choices.

Changes in Routine/Control

You feel as if you need to be in control of your environment and your baby; a change in plans that is not structured to what you have become accustomed to can be very upsetting. This is furthered by the fact that the NICU was such a structured environment.

Posttraumatic Stress Disorder

Posttraumatic stress disorder is a draining condition that develops from a life-threatening or terrifying event. In the case of a preemie, the event is usually the birth or the events in the NICU immediately following the birth. A person who is experiencing posttraumatic stress disorder will continue to have frightening thoughts and memories of the ordeal that she has gone through. The symptoms of PTSD may develop within a few weeks or not until years after. This anxiety also has the ability to appear and disappear. Symptoms of posttraumatic stress disrorder include:

Reliving the Event

You may find that you have intrusive thoughts that make it seem as if the event is happening all over again. A person may relive the event through smells, images, memories, nightmares, or flashbacks.

Cannot Sleep

You have difficulty sleeping, feel restless, and may be afraid of the nightmares or flashbacks.

Emotionally Numb or Detached

A parent may feel frustrated that she cannot change the situation and feel numb or detached from the baby. You may find that you are building protective walls around yourself out of fear.

Loss of Interest

Things that used to be of interest to you are no longer enjoyable. You may also find yourself less affectionate. As a result of the traumatic event, you will avoid people, places, or things associated with the event.

More Aggressive/Violent

Many people experience intense irritability and may become more aggressive, even violent, in a situation where a threat is perceived.

Panic

Panic is the sudden strong feeling of fear that prevents you from reasonable thought or action. Panic can have very real physical symptoms, including chest and muscle tension, shortness of breath, sweating, rapid heartbeat, dizziness, numbness, tingling, and other muscular aches. An onslaught of some or all of these symptoms can also be referred to as a panic attack or anxiety attack. These attacks are twice as common in women. Untreated, they can become very incapacitating. Panic disorders can also be accompanied by other disorders. If you are suffering physical symptoms, you should have yourself checked by a medical professional.

Specific Phobias

An extreme irrational fear of something specific. It could be blood, needles, procedures, rooms, or places. It is an intense fear of something that is usually a threat or danger. The fear brings about specific physical stressors including panic attacks.

Obsessive Compulsive Disorder

As it relates to the parenting of a premature infant, Obsessive Compulsive Disorder (OCD) usually refers to actions involving the care of the baby. OCD are the feelings, thoughts, or images that if you do not do something, it will end in a negative result. What the negative result will be can be known or unknown.

Other forms of Obsessive Compulsive Disorder can include:

Excessive Fear of Germs or Contamination

This is a realistic fear as it relates to a preemie. You were trained in the NICU on the extreme measures that were needed to ensure that your baby was not exposed to germs or contamination, so you have good reason to fear exposure to germs or contamination. An exaggerated response to fear of germs by excessive hand washing, wearing masks, and not allowing the baby to be exposed to normal activities may be viewed as an excessive fear.

Checking the Baby

Keep in mind that OCD is to the extreme. Checking your baby is expected and encouraged. However, if you find yourself checking the baby more often or having unrealistic fears of what will happen if you do not check the baby or doubting what you have just seen, then you may be going to extremes. Checking the baby can also mean a constant review of the baby's anatomy to see if you can find any hint of developing disease.

The Constant Need for Assurances

Are you sure the baby is ok? Are you sure she got the right amount of medication? Frequent and disturbing thoughts about the care of yourself, your environment, or the baby can be a form of OCD.

PRACTICAL EXERCISES TO ELIMINATE EXCESSIVE ANXIETY

While you may or may not have recognized the symptoms of what you have been feeling over the past weeks or months, the bigger question becomes: How do I control these thoughts and feelings while some of the stressors in my life continue? The baby may still need constant attention; there may still be ongoing medical needs and even if there are not medical needs now, there is always the fear of what the future will hold for your baby. While these exercises offer a you a practical way to respond to the stress, it is still a good idea to be evaluated by a mental health professional if you are unable to resolve your symptoms. Some forms of anxiety require careful diagnostic evaluation as there may be other co-existing conditions. Unmanageable forms of anxiety can require medication and psychotherapy. There are also a number of support groups that are available.

The exercises included here are based on the Cognitive Behavioral Model of therapy. The behavioral component seeks to change your re-actions to anxiety-provoking situations. They also may include relaxation and coping strategies. In order to be effective you must target your specific anxieties; the first step in treating them is to identify them. Using the same Reality Rules identified in chapter 4 you can specifically pinpoint the anxiety-provoking thoughts and the level to which they effect your daily functioning. Identify what causes your anxiety.

Now that you have identified those thoughts that cause you increased anxiety, try using the following:

Decrease Negative Thinking

Negative thoughts are destructive and put a damper on any happy, positive, or satisfying thoughts. If you do think a happy thought it is usually immediately replaced by an unhappy thought. This pattern of thinking lessens your chances of being happy. It is well accepted that you cannot control this thinking; it comes automatically. What you can do is to question the negative thought. As you find yourself thinking negatively about a specific instance, recognize the thought and analyze the thought to see if there is any truth in it. You can also take that same negative thought and spin it into all of the most positive things that can come from it. While this sounds like an easy task it is not. When you have developed a pattern of negative thinking it will be difficult to find the positive.

Change Your Vocabulary

Pay attention to the words you use, and stop yourself from using "should have," "might have," "if only," and "what if." Accept words such as "it is," "I am," and "I did" to recognize the reality of what has already happened or been done; phrases listed above only leave an open door for false ideas.

Get Out

Leave your house, leave your safe place. Experience new people and places. By getting out you are giving your mind the time to re-focus on other events or themes that may not be anxiety-provoking. Go for a walk, go to the mall, see a movie, visit a friend. You have had a baby; share your joy with the world. The fresh air will do you both good. Sunshine promotes growth.

Exposure

Expose yourself slowly to those things that provoke your anxiety. If you are afraid to take the baby out of the house, sit out on the front porch as a start and slowly go farther and farther from the house; soon you will be walking around the block. By exposing yourself to the anxiety trigger you are able to tolerate and recognize that nothing bad is going to happen.

Develop a Pattern of Relaxation

We all have our "special place." This may be literally a place that we go or even just a thought of something. The most important aspect of your "special place" is that it provides serenity and relaxation. Visualize yourself doing what is most relaxing for you; try muscle relaxation and breathing exercises or spiritual pursuits. Some people find that having someone to talk to is a form of relaxing.

Diet and Exercise

Diet and exercise are a significant part of how our bodies function. You have spent the past weeks or months in a hospital setting. You have probably been lacking in exercise and your choice of foods in a hospital is limited. Diet and exercise cannot only transform your body, they can transform your mind. Limit your intake of unhealthy fat and refined sugar. At the same time you should increase your fresh fruits, grains, and vegetables. Caffeine and alcohol can be anxiety-provoking triggers; use them in moderation. If exercising is not part of your normal routine, do it in moderation: a walk around the block, a swim in the pool. Exercise is not only a source of stress relief, it also does wonders in calming your thoughts.

EXHAUSTION PHASE

While you are still experiencing the stress of bringing home your baby, you are also ending a chapter that began in the hospital. You changed every aspect of your being from your emotions to your daily routines and now it is coming to an end. During that Adaptation Phase in part you were running on adrenaline. While your mind is moving on to the next phase of parenting this preemie, your body may not respond in the same way. It is during this time that you will find that the third and final phase of the General Adaptation Syndrome begin to appear, the Exhaustion Phase. You have dealt with all of the stressors and been vigilant in monitoring your baby's care and now your body and mind are experiencing some of the aftershock.

Exhaustion is reaching the bottom of the barrel, there is no more to give. If you find that you feel as if you are about to crash, you must make yourself a priority. There is nothing to feel ashamed of; the stress has overcome your body and you will recover. However, failure to react to your body's signals that you are exhausted can result in physical ailments having long-term effects. During this exhaustion phase your body's immune system is much more susceptible to disease and infection.

These milestones should be used as a guideline in the development of your preemie. As a parent and daily care giver to your baby, you will be confident in your assessment of your child and her continuing development. In addition, there will be ongoing medical providers or maybe just your pediatrician who will be able to assess and intervene if necessary to make sure that your baby is on the right path.

Remember even if your baby does have developmental delays this is not cause for panic. There are a number of interventions that can be taken to provide corrective measures.

Chapter 12

Inspiration and Hope

There are not two women in this world who will share the same experience in parenting a preemie. What you will share is a myriad of emotions that are similar to those who have lived through the experience. We hope that by sharing their stories, you will find that same inspiration and hope that has helped them in their journeys of parenting a preemie.

ZOE'S EARLY ARRIVAL

By Amy Marquis

Having a preemie is the hardest thing I have ever done. I had led a charmed life up to that point—no major challenges to face, a loving family, a good education, and money for whatever I needed.

Maybe that is why, even when I began to spot at 17 weeks of pregnancy, I was not that worried. Obviously, it was disturbing to see the spotting, but I had heard that a lot of women spot. It did not occur to me that Zoe could come so early or that it would be so difficult if she did.

By the fifth episode, I knew that my body meant to kick her out. At just 29 weeks' gestation, my little girl was going to have to fight her way to full-term development on the outside. Without my protection. I had waited my whole life to become a mother, and now I had failed my daughter before she had even been born.

Labor went quickly because of the spotting. They barely had time to give me an epidural before Zoe was born. And although I was grateful for the relief at the time, I now understand why women elect to go through natural childbirth. The epidural put me in a fog. I was so sleepy that by the time I made it to the delivery room, I was ready for a nap, and I could not tell if I was pushing hard enough. In some ways I feel robbed of the experience of seeing my daughter being born. I had made it through several days of contractions and my entire labor naturally. If I had pushed myself, I could have borne the pain of going through all the way without drugs. Still, they served their purpose.

Zoe was born, and she barely made a sound. They rushed her off to hook her up to a ventilator, so I did not get to hold her. I was not even allowed to see her precious face until hours later. But the drugs numbed that pain, too.

Now that she had arrived, I had no time for depression. Or maybe it was simply my way of coping—in the midst of a crisis, hopelessness was a luxury I could not afford. Although I did not consciously make that decision, when I look back, I think my denial saved me. It kept me from falling apart when my baby needed me most. As the mother of a preemie, I had duties to attend to. The first was to visit my new daughter in the intensive care nursery as often as possible without tiring her out. The second was something no one else could do for Zoe, not even the nurses who tended to her every need.

I had always planned to breast-feed, and when I learned how vulnerable Zoe was, I was even more determined. All preemies are robbed of the last trimester of pregnancy, and that is when a baby's immune system gains most of its strength. Without breast milk, which carries antibodies that cannot be passed in any other way, the immune system is compromised even further. As a preemie mom, my milk was different from the breast milk of full-term moms. It had more fat and calories and a greater concentration of immunities. But there was a catch: Babies do not develop their ability to feed by mouth until 34 weeks' gestation. Zoe was 29 weeks. That meant I would have to use a substitute to establish and sustain my milk supply, and so I bought the most powerful breast pump I could find. This siphoning machine looked something like a medieval torture device, but when it was used faithfully, every three hours, it extracted a miracle: liquid gold . . . mother's milk.

My first bounty was a full three milliliters, the exact amount the nurse needed for Zoe's first official feeding. I was on top of the world. Now that my milk ducts were cooperating, Zoe's fragile stomach, which was already performing tasks it was never meant to do this early in life by digesting, would never have to struggle with synthetic formula, and her immune system would get a much needed boost. The days passed in a frenzy of pumping sessions, thorough bottle washing after each pumping, and visits to the nursery. I was so tired. I had the fatigue of a new mother without the actual baby in my care. Waking up two times a night to pump quickly became tiring, unfulfilling, and downright depressing, but I pressed on because I was a mother now. Pumping was the only thing that made me feel like I had earned the title.

Zoe was so delicate, so small. I felt a pang of guilt as I thought about how the mere force of gravity was a burden on Zoe. She was not ready for it. She should not be expected to bear it so soon, I thought. The plates in her head formed a ridge on her forehead. If she was lying on the right side of her face, the ridge appeared along the left side of her forehead. The nurse said that was because her plates had not yet fused.

The IV was the hardest thing to see. Zoe's veins were so tiny, and that needle was cruelly jammed into her arm, which was splinted to keep the needle from popping out. The tape that held it in place was wrapped so tightly that it dug into my sweet baby girl's skin.

Even the temperature of the room was too much for Zoe. She had to be placed in a heated isolette because her body could not regulate its own temperature. I wanted so much to hold her, but every time I took her out of her plastic womb, I knew I was risking her body temperature falling. Much of the time, I was forced to watch my daughter the same way I would gaze at a beautiful tropical fish in its tank.

Full-term newborns have to adjust to their new surroundings, and it is a big shock. My brave, innocent baby had to endure so much more. It was my fault she had been brought into this world so early. My fault she had to be incubated because her lungs were not ready to breathe on their own. My fault she had to have her IV changed every couple of days. My fault her eyes were solid black because her irises had not had time to develop before her arrival. My fault she could have learning disabilities later in life. My fault that the way she perceives pain could be affected for the rest of her life because of all she was enduring now.

Most mothers declare that they would recognize their newborns anywhere, but I did not have a good feel for what Zoe's face looked like because she was intubated. She was not capable of feeding by mouth yet as she was only a 29-weeker, so she was fed through a tube that was threaded through her tiny nostril and into her stomach. There were several sensor pads that covered a good portion of her chest. They fed vital information to the heart and pulse-ox monitors so the nurse would know if Zoe had apnea or bradycardia, which were called "As and Bs" for short. Apnea is when the baby stops breathing; bradycardia is when the baby's heart stops, the nurse told me. My husband and I were getting a terrifying education that no parents should be privy to.

The nurse taught us how to touch Zoe's sensitive body. Preemies have very thin skin, she explained, so even though it is counterintuitive, stroking Zoe is more irritating than it is soothing. And so we learned to place our hands firmly on her tiny crown and along the bottoms of her tiny feet to "contain" her, make her feel more like she was still inside my womb. It saddened me beyond words to think that we had to simulate the conditions of my womb for her. And that this nurse, this woman I had never seen before, knew more about my baby than I did. She had spent more time with her than I had. Did Zoe think of her as her mother? That very question seared my soul and made me feel more impotent than I had ever felt in my life. And even though that nurse and the rest who came after her were responsible for sustaining Zoe's life, I would resent them throughout our NICU stay.

Meanwhile, the hospital had discharged me on the third day after Zoe was born. It was the hardest day of my life. Once I started crying, I could not stop. Many months later, I read that the third day after birth is when a postpartum woman's hormones are at their highest levels. Looking back, my indescribable misery made even more sense.

During the next five weeks, everyone wanted to come visit us in the hospital, or they wanted us to call with updates. In the heart of a crisis it is a tall order to accommodate visitors and make small talk with concerned relatives. Every second I was on the phone meant time away from Zoe. Or time I was supposed to be pumping so my milk supply would remain well established for her. Or at the very least it was time I could use to catch up on sleep. And if someone showed up for a visit during Zoe's feeding time, I was forced to socialize instead of bonding with my daughter, which I only got the opportunity to do a few hours a day because she was sleeping the rest of the time. I knew people were trying to be nice, but I just wanted to be left alone. When Zoe came home, they could call and visit all they liked. What I needed more than anything was my meals to be cooked or my laundry to be done, but a precious few picked up on that.

The weeks dragged on until, finally, the doctors said those magic words: "It's time for Zoe to go home."

Her homecoming was joyous and challenging because the journey of a preemie is not over once you leave the hospital. Keeping watch for developmental concerns was a huge burden. And there were big bad viruses looming that every preemie parent lives in fear of—RSV can be life threatening. So for the first year of Zoe's life we washed our hands until they were raw, made visitors do the same, and rarely left the house during the winter in order to keep her safe from those nasty germs. That time with Zoe was an isolating one, both practically and emotionally. Few could understand what we faced, and that was frustrating. Once Zoe was out of the hospital, even family members thought we should move on—that she should be treated like any other baby and not a preemie. But we held our ground. We knew we had to protect Zoe's body, that it simply was not ready to face the outside world. Nobody wanted to hear about our fears and worries. I think hearing those things made them feel uncomfortable. It was trying not to have anyone to talk to in an honest way. But as Zoe grew stronger, we gradually opened up and moved forward with our lives.

We just celebrated Zoe's third birthday. She has overcome all the challenges in her way and is a very healthy child. Maybe it is because of her rough start that she has a great attitude about life. She is happy as can be. When Zoe was born, I was filled with worry and shame because I felt responsible for all that my daughter had to overcome. The guilt that came from my body failing Zoe was a heavy burden, one that I carry still. Like most painful things, time lessens its power. But more than that, I think seeing Zoe grow into a thriving person, one with thoughts and feelings and extraordinary abilities, helps to keep my guilt at bay. My body may have failed me, but my love has not. Now I am more proud of her than words can say. Every accomplishment she has made—crawling, walking, her first words and beyond—is that much more amazing and precious to me. She is truly my miracle.

NATHANIEL J.'S JOURNEY
By Janet Norris

My name is Janet, and I am the mother of a son who was born at 30.5 weeks. He is now almost five years old. While we continue to struggle with the effects of having a premature infant, we know how blessed we are to have overcome this traumatic experience with such positive feelings. It seems like just yesterday that my pregnancy left me on complete bed rest at seven weeks pregnant. I very quickly became scared, with my thoughts racing about what might be. A great friend of mine gently showered me with religious literature. With the literature she provided the advice to protect my mind and guard my heart. Confused at what this meant, I put reading the literature on hold.

After six weeks of nothing but lying in bed, I ventured out of bed, my shaky legs barely carrying me to the lower level of my home. It was then I greeted God, when I begged for understanding and filled the air with a stream of spontaneous questions. I wanted answers as to why my pregnancy was in jeopardy. I somehow blamed myself and begged God to grant me forgiveness for my sins and pleaded for his approval in this pregnancy by granting me the child I was carrying. At the time the emotional suffering I felt could be compared to no pain I had ever experienced before. In my darkest moment I asked God to take this child now if it was his plan because my suffering was more than I could bear. As I thought of my words to God and my thoughts of despair, my greatest fear was now that God might grant that wish and that I would have to tell my husband what I had asked God to do. What kind of person could be so selfish? What if my child died now because I asked God to end my suffering? Not knowing where to turn and feeling a tremendous amount of guilt for my thoughts, I headed upstairs and dusted off the literature my friend had left for me. After all, my mind certainly was not protected, and my heart was not guarded.

I spent the next three weeks rebuilding my relationship with God. After almost nine weeks on total bed rest, my challenge of maintaining this pregnancy stopped. In an instant it was gone. As quickly as the bleeding began, it had ended, almost as if a spigot had been turned off.

The next several weeks continued on a normal path. My only challenge now was how to consume enough ice and not live with my derrière connected to the toilet. It seems the extent of my pica was for ice. I had heard of various degrees of craving nonfood items, such as drywall, dirt, sand, and even wanting to consume cleaning products. I do not think I will ever understand what makes an expectant mother crave nonfood items.

At 30.3 weeks' gestation, I stopped physically urinating. Yes, I stopped urinating altogether since all the fluid I consumed went to replacing the amniotic fluid I was leaking and was not coming out as waste. Then, in a flash, it appeared that my son was pushing on my bladder. The urine was anything but—it was amniotic fluid. I was admitted to the hospital, where I would remain for the next nine weeks, or until the birth of my son, Nathaniel.

While the next two days seemed to crawl, I felt an overwhelming connection to God. I could hear him in my heart and in my mind. I even recalled a dream I had where a very special messenger told me that things would be rough, but to trust God and that all will be fine in the end.

I felt a warm confidence that all truly would be fine in the end. I never lost that confidence during each test, shot, exam, and ultrasound. I had peace in my soul. I was given the reassurance through my own soul searching to look for the positive while God dealt with the rest. I was not seeing the negative of his lungs not fully developed or all the other possible dangers of having a premature baby.

It was during these two days that I developed a condition I like to call "mama bear syndrome": a natural instinct to protect and guard what is yours without regard for yourself. Although I had peace in my soul for my son's birth, I started to get very demanding about ensuring that the best care would be given to my child. My instincts told me that my baby was getting the proper nutrients from just an IV, but I needed to have some substance enter my mouth. An attendant agreed to give me ice chips and his dinner. After all, it was in the middle of the night. I never felt so grateful for ice before in my life. I felt as if I had literally hit the lottery. I had ice, and I was grateful. Despite the fact that I was half-starved and had the food in front of me, my instinct to protect my child and follow the doctors' orders prevailed, and I did not eat.

I sat up that night talking to the resident about my inner peace. I confessed my fears but still wanted to have my child naturally, the way moms have done for centuries. His attempts to calm my fears fell on deaf ears. I was not hearing him.

At 30.5 weeks' gestation, Nathaniel J. Dale (J stands for Jesus) entered into this world at four pounds two ounces, and 18 inches long. Immediately after delivery, they placed him on my stomach. It was like seeing an angel on my belly, and the warmth of God was already filling my heart. What was expected to be a difficult labor was five contractions lasting 18 minutes, and the result was a natural childbirth experience. I did not endure the physical pain that most women experience in childbirth, but I endured more emotional pain than I would want anyone to have to experience.

When Nathaniel was ready to be transported to another hospital with a state-of-the-art NICU, I was given the choice of going with him and being under another doctor's care or staying where I was for one day. I decided I would stay so that I could recover. The experience has been both physically and emotionally draining. Less than 22 hours after giving birth, I was discharged from the hospital, picked up my breast pump, went home to six loads of laundry, and still managed to spend eight hours at the NICU that night. The next 21 days flew by. I had missed so much of my third trimester. I had a room to prepare, items to buy (after all, my shower had not come yet), and doctors to research. The nurses were amazed at my recovery and disposition about my child's health. What they did not know was that I had full faith in God and trusted my faith and his will to overcome any obstacles in my son's health.

After four and a half years, I can still feel shortchanged from a long and fat pregnancy, especially since my body would only tolerate one pregnancy. At first it was not easy to accept losing a major part of the third trimester, Lamaze, the hospital tour, and feeling my baby kick. There are times when it still hurts to know that I was given that one chance, and only one. What keeps me smiling is when I see my little angel looking at me, hugging me, loving me—all that pain magically disappears. Each and every day, I see the blessings that God has given to me. I stopped counting those blessings and now pray that someone else finds comfort in my story. I truly am blessed. My advice to all parents suffering through a challenging pregnancy or parenting a baby in the NICU is to have faith.

THE LITTLE RED DRESS OF HOPE

By Kimberly Hall

I gave birth to my baby girl, Angel, at 25 weeks on June 7, 2000. She weighed 1 pound 11.3 ounces and was 12 and one-quarter inches long. I had an emergency cesarean section and did not get to see my little girl until the following day. Angel had many ups and downs in the NICU. One of her many issues was weight gain and feeding.

On June 8, 2000, the nurses helped me out of bed. I was sore and could hardly move but anxiously waited to see Angel for the first time. My husband helped me dress. I remember feeling so nervous. I had lost a baby boy eight months prior and just could not bear the pain of losing another. The NICU doctor had come to see us earlier in the morning, and the things he had told us had me shaky and scared. I clung to the fact that she had made it through the night, but I knew that she was still critical. While I recognize that doctors need to be realistic, I remember hating him for even thinking—not only telling me—that I should not get my hopes up. I knew as soon as I saw her that she was going to live. How could he not see that she was a fighter, already kicking and showing her spirit?

Unfortunately, all my optimism started to sour as the days went on. I worried more and more. By the fifth day, my Angel had lost a significant amount of weight and was not tolerating her feedings. The baby next to Angel, Alexandra, looked so big, and I secretly wished that my baby was that big. The mother of Alexandra did not realize how lucky she was. I never met her because she never came to see her baby. However, the grandmother of Alexandra was there faithfully every day, showering that baby with love. I came to share my hopes and fears with her and quickly realized that despite the hopelessness, I felt now that there was a light at the end of the tunnel. Alexandra's grandmother shared with me that Alexandra also was born weighing 1 pound 12 ounces and now weighed 3 pounds at two months of age. She was even learning to nipple feed. This kind woman shared her fears for her granddaughter, and I was both sad and joyful as Alexandra left the NICU. As a parting gift to me, Alexandra's grandmother gave me a little red doll dress, which had been passed on to her by a preemie mom the day Alexandra was born. The dress had literally belonged to a baby doll and compared to my baby, it looked disproportionate. She referred to it as the little red dress of hope, and while the dress itself was nothing more than cloth, it represented hope. It was a reminder to me that Alexandra and the baby before her had made it through all the ups and downs of the NICU.

While in the beginning I was having difficulty seeing anything positive in the NICU or about my baby's medical condition, it seemed that there was always something beeping or alarming and sending shear panic waves through my body. In June, my worst fears came true—all the beeps and alarms I had been assured were normal resulted in my baby having to be resuscitated. She was now holding on to life with the assistance of a machine. I held that little red dress as if it were God himself and prayed, bargained, and pleaded with the Almighty to let her live. Then, just as suddenly as she had crashed, she began to regain her strength and her weight, and all I could do was cry. My tears were of joy, for the fact she was alive, and fear for what was to come.

In August, Angel finally outgrew that little red dress of hope. The dress had served as a reminder of hope, a cloth for my tears and the joy I felt as she outgrew it. While in the back of my mind I knew that this dress had nothing to do with the progress my child had made, I knew that it was a crutch that helped me in making it through. I passed that little red dress on to Ashley, a 24-weeker weighing just one pound five ounces, and she passed it on from there. My hope is that that little red dress, or whatever token of hope the parents of the NICU find, helps to provide encouragement and strength in the toughest of times.

TIME WELL SPENT WITH JILLIE AND CASSIE

By Tamala Moore

I am a mother that had a seven-month experience in the NICU; three months in the first hospital, and then, flown by helicopter, at another hospital, where we stayed for four more months. It has been a hard experience, to say the least. But it was an experience that I would go through again to gain the beautiful, vibrant child that is my daughter, Jillian.

I started out with two daughters, identical twins named Jillian Rose and Cassidy Fay. It stabs me every day that we lost Cassie. I know I said I would go through the whole experience again, but if I could just remove the part of losing Cassie. Complications from the identical twin gestation put me on bed rest at home at 21 weeks; by

24 weeks I was admitted into antipartum. Thank God I received steroid injections to mature their lungs because I had an emergency cesarean section at 27 weeks. I am sure this is why their lungs were strong enough to be extubated on their second day. Jillian was 2 pounds even, and Cassidy was 1 pound 14 ounces.

The babies were whisked away to the NICU. I was wheeled in on a bed to see them for the first time with my husband. They were so tiny, so still, so out of their element; hooked up to all kinds of wires, breathing machines, under bright lights with tiny masks over their eyes, wearing the tiniest little diapers that were still so big on them. It looked like something you would see on television, not something that would ever happen to your own babies. It was so surreal. I remember I felt so disconnected from them, like they were not my babies, not my girls that were growing inside of me just a few short hours ago. I remember thinking, what is wrong with me? Why is my soul not singing from seeing my babies for the first time? What kind of mother am I? I guess it was nerves because I threw up right there in the NICU.

On later reflection I think those feelings of disconnection were some kind of psychological cushion or a sort of posttraumatic stress. I remember I also felt disconnected from myself. As soon as my catheter was removed and I could get out of bed, I went to the NICU to see my babies. It was a mixture of emotions, but the feelings of disconnection had worn off. I was amazed by them, in love, saw them as so beautiful, tiny versions of perfection; yet my heart broke in half at the same time because for one thing, they were torn apart from each other, when in the womb, they had been so close that one would put her head on the other's chest, and second, there was no turning back, what was done was done, and this was their reality. I kicked myself, and still do to this day, for not getting a second opinion before they were taken.

Acceptance set in; there was nothing I could do to change it. I decided to focus on the happiness that I could finally meet my babies. So I filled my days by their isolettes, spending equal time with each baby, kangaroo-care holding them, singing and talking softly to them, placing my hand on them, just letting them know that Mommy was there and trying to give them what little sense of familiarity I could, the familiarity and comfort that only their mother could give them. My instincts told me that they needed to feel my presence. And Lord knows for myself I needed to feel theirs. I spent the days by sending out their birth announcements, pumping breast milk, and just sitting there in a rocking chair with swollen feet.

When they were four days old, I knew something was wrong with Jillian—I could see it in her face. I somehow knew she was in pain. I told the doctors that something was wrong with her. It was dismissed. A few days later, it was confirmed that Jillian had a brain bleed, a grade 4, the worst possible. Oddly enough, I swear that during that time I had an excruciating headache like I had never had in my life. Call me weird, but I swear I was picking up on her pain. I was told that she would be a cerebral palsy child, would be in a wheelchair, would not walk or talk. I remember thinking, how would she feel her whole life being how she was and seeing an exact replica of herself doing everything she could not? I kept my thoughts positive, refusing to believe it was a definite, and focused on the idea that we would help her retrain her little brain to compensate for the damaged part. As it turned out, I was right, because every day, Jillian is closer to being a normal child. She is beating the odds.

Two weeks went by, and on a Wednesday, Cassidy, who was skating right through, always the calm, serene one, handling everything like a trooper, got sick. The night before, her little eyes were open and she was looking right at me, so serenely, pursing her little lips, holding my finger with so much strength in her little hand. She showed no signs that a fatal hand-passed bacteria was brewing in her little body. She died on Thursday in my arms after a horrible battle, the same day the birth announcements arrived in everyone's mailboxes. If I could only go back and let her have gone peacefully instead of all that was done to her for hours before they disconnected her. But I believed until literally the last minute that she was going to turn around any minute and be a miracle. But I know today that if I had not allowed them to do everything, I would have questioned myself for the rest of my life. She did have a few minutes of loving peacefulness with us before her heart stopped. There is not a day that goes by that I do not feel a huge hole.

Immediately, Jillian also ended up with a bacteria that caused necrotizing enterocolitis; she remained very sick for two weeks, was reintubated, and finally needed surgery to remove part of her intestines. She recovered from the surgery well. A month later, she was going to go home but started having sever diarrhea. But Jillie was full of fight, screaming to be fed. I was told by others that I ought to question the doctors. I did question the doctors. Jillie went another two weeks without any food. When it happened again a month later, I nicely insisted on transferring her. My suggestion met with some resistance, but I would not take no for an answer. I am glad I persisted and trusted my instincts to transfer her because it ended up that she was misdiagnosed. Even doctors are not perfect.

A month after the transfer, she needed another surgery because of a stricture resulting from the first surgery. Even the best hospitals have bacteria that can reach your baby through their access lines. Thus I cannot stress sanitation enough, for yourself and for the staff as well. I made sure my hands were always sanitized before touching Jillian. If I just touched the chair, I made sure I sanitized my hands before touching her again.

I know everyone's experience is different and of all different calibers. In my experience I started out with blind trust in all the medical staff, just standing in the background. But because of the roller coaster that Jillian went through, and the loss of one child already, I became vigilant and assertive about my remaining daughter's care. I asked to be present for the daily doctors' rounds when they discussed her. I began a journal, keeping notes on everything every day, from her temperature to her heart rate to her sats. Anything, large or small, that applied to her, I wrote down. It ended up being invaluable. The doctors and nurses began to respect my input, encouraged it even, realizing that nobody knew my baby like I did, and included me in the decision making for her. I educated myself about her medical conditions. Actually, it just becomes second nature when you are there, living it, every day.

But I must say that my constant presence was not appreciated by all the nursing staff. Some nurses are quite appreciative of a mother that is always present and asks intelligent questions about the progress of her baby; they realize that it is in the best interest of the baby. But there are others who feel that such a mother is obtrusive and who feel that her presence is hovering. I dealt with this by thinking that the ones that did not want me there would forget all about me in a year, whereas if I was not with my baby and something happened, I would never forget it or forgive myself for the rest of my life. I could not have handled losing another precious child.

You are told at the beginning to expect a roller coaster of emotions as you go through the NICU experience with your baby. How true this is. One day, your world is happy: Your baby is making progress and having a good day. In an instant, everything can crumble because she starts showing signs of yet another problem, and the roller coaster plummets as you are scared for her life again. You feel so helpless sometimes. You cannot protect her from the world like you are supposed to. You know something painful is going to happen, and your hands are tied because you have to allow it. You long for the day of simple stubbed toes and scraped knees. Yet at the same time, while you *must* remain positive that she is coming home one day—you *must* remain optimistic—you still have that gnawing fear: What if she dies?

You go home to spend the night and sit in your baby's nursery and cry because you know you could not handle it if this room stayed empty. In my case we had already removed one crib. I was fortunate to have a huge support structure. I know the NICU experience can either bring you closer to your spouse or it can tear your relationship up, but I was fortunate that it bonded my husband and I like never before. As we all know, men are not as expressive as women, and he did not have much to say in words, but his constant support spoke volumes that words could not. My mother was my backbone. If I took my mother for granted before becoming a mother myself, her constant support solidified in my eyes just what a mother will do for her child. She spent countless nights with Jillian in my stead, shooing me away to go get sleep or go home to visit my husband, was there for every surgery, major or minor, and stood up like a mama bear protecting her little cubs. She felt everything I felt and rode that emotional roller coaster with me. She and my husband gave me my stamina and strength. People are there for you like never before. Friends and family call, leaving messages of love and encouragement that can lift you up a little on a particularly bad day. Even complete strangers around the country kept tabs on Jillian through various friends. This rough time helped me to see the humanity in the world, especially how people can reach out; but it also helped me to remember not to judge other people if they seem particularly rude or withdrawn because you never know what they have gone through themselves in their own lives.

Finally, the day came when Jillian came home. She was seven months old and only weighed five and a half pounds. She looked like a chicken with no feathers. She was so skinny, and her ears did not fit her head. She had a feeding tube that I learned to take care of and was hooked up to an apnea monitor, keeping track of her heart rate and respiration. It was the happiest day and the scariest day of my life. I remember feelings of being overwhelmed with fear. There were times I would cry because I was afraid to be alone with her. Now it was just me, and I was so afraid I would do something to jeopardize her. I questioned myself constantly.

But the minute she came home, I could almost feel her take a deep breath and relax. She flourished at home. She put on three and a half pounds in seven months in the hospital, but she put on three and a half pounds in seven weeks at home. Every day, her color got better. She was smiling and cooing. Her feeding tube came out after three months. Away went the apnea monitor. I started calling her Bean Sprout because she was growing like a weed.

Now she is almost a normal little girl. I say almost because her development is delayed. But she gets considerable therapy, which is of the utmost importance. I also work with her constantly, trying to help her keep within developmental milestones, but she just thinks of it as play. To this day, there are latent psychological issues with me. Just recently, her ophthalmologist wanted to do eye surgery to release the muscles in one of her eyes because her eye is drifting inward. Even though it is a simple outpatient procedure, just hearing the word *surgery* in his office made me tear up. I have lightened up considerably, but there are times, many times, when I am overprotective of her for fear that I might let one little thing slip and lose her, as unrealistic as that is. But I am convinced that Jillian is going to succeed, and has already.

I love my little Jillie Bean, and I would go through that trying time all over again to have what I have right now, sleeping in her crib, knowing that in the morning I get to wake up to smiles and giggles and a look in her eyes that says I am her whole world. I get to be a mommy.

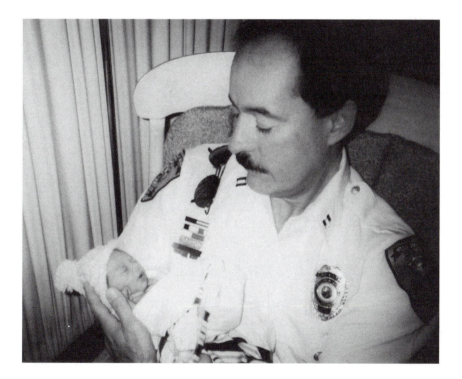

Chapter 13

What Happens to Dad

For every woman that has a baby, there is a man out there somewhere. There is very little literature on what men feel when a pregnancy ends unexpectedly. Even more unusual is that despite the fact that there are just as many fathers as there are mothers, all the Web sites and organizations that have made a special place for fathers get very little activity. While the women experience the raw emotions that come with having a preterm baby, the men are almost left out in the cold emotionally and in the support they receive. This, coupled with society's customary response that the man is supposed to be the strong one, or that "men don't cry," makes it no surprise that men do not feel comfortable sharing their emotions in this situation. Some men would consider showing any signs of emotion as weakness.

SHARING MY PARTNER

Studies have shown that married men tend to live longer and report more overall satisfaction than unmarried men. Men also admit to enjoying being the one and only. This feeling of being the one and only is common for men in both preterm and full-term pregnancies. Men in general like the idea of primariness, and bringing a baby into the picture means that he will be sharing his partner, her time, her attention, and even her body. While this can be stressful, at the same time, the feelings can evoke a sense of guilt about his feelings of resentment. This is contrary to a woman's feelings. A woman does usually feel stressed because she must share her spouse with her child. She views her spouse and her as sharing the child.

When the pregnancy is high risk, a man's feelings are compounded because the man is so removed, not only from the woman, but from the progression of the pregnancy. This is not intentional, but the focus of the physician is the patients: mother and baby. Sometimes even physicians fail to recognize the important role that the father can play in progressing through a difficult pregnancy.

NO REST FOR DAD

While a woman is on bed rest, it becomes the primary responsibility of the father to take care of the children and all the household chores that go along with it. If the mother has been confined to bed rest, then her activities will be limited. Even if she is not confined to the bed, she may not be able to lift the smallest of objects, including other children.

Should she be confined to the bed, this will take an emotional toll on all members of the family. Being isolated in a room by yourself while the rest of the family functions is extremely difficult. As the father, you may be the sole link to the adult outside world. Despite all the added responsibilities, she will probably want your attention when you are not working or doing those extra activities. While she has an excessive amount of solitude, a father will likely have very little. While a father is making every attempt to hold things together and be supportive of the baby's mother, he may also be exposed to the emotional mood swings that pregnant women are so well known for. The emotions can sometimes be compounded with the added stress of being confined to a bed.

It is also a time when many people, including family and health care providers, to some extent shut the father out. The focus is on the baby and the mother. Sometimes from the beginning of the pregnancy until the end, no one will ever ask the father how he is doing. Those questions are usually directed toward the mother: "How's your wife? How's the baby?" The situation, pre- or postbirth, becomes frustrating, and many men find themselves emotionally shutting down.

YOUR SEX LIFE

If you are dealing with a high-risk or complicated pregnancy, your sex life might be the first thing you lose. Many complications require a woman to abstain from intercourse. Some women are even told that orgasms can produce complications in an already high-risk pregnancy.

As a man, while you are still able to function, you may not have the desire to ask your wife to satisfy your needs when she is not allowed to let you do the same for her. The lack of sex in the relationship can contribute to stress. It also has an impact on the level of intimacy that you feel toward each other. The lack of the sense of closeness that existed based on your sexual relationship can make you feel more distant than normal. While sexual acts may be limited, you can still create romance and intimacy in the bedroom, knowing that she will be back to her old self after the baby is born. A sense of intimacy can help both partners in recognizing that the relationship has not changed and is just progressing to a deeper level with the creation of a new life.

STAY INVOLVED

As the pregnancy progresses, a woman will develop an increasingly strong bond with her medical provider. After all, she is trusting her safety and the safety of her baby to this person. Some women have described this as feeling like there was "another man" in their lives. The question becomes, where does Dad fit into this picture? The answer is simple, and your role is indispensable: You are an advocate for your partner. While most medical providers will gladly answer any questions and your partner is more than likely keeping you apprized of the latest details of the baby's progression, you still may feel a disconnect. The more doctors' visits and other important appointments you attend, the more involved you will feel. It is important that you understand the information. You may be forced to make decisions without being able to consult your partner, for example, if she is under anesthesia. The pregnancy is high risk, and you may have to make some decisions without time to discuss or research your options. It is important that as a partner and father of the baby, you are confident that you are making the choices that are best for your family. Let all the parties involved, including doctors, hospital staff, and specialists, be aware that you are an integral part of the process.

YOUR EMOTIONS

While men do not experience the pregnancy physically, they still may find themselves experiencing similar emotions, such as anger, frustration, denial, fear, helplessness, guilt, and depression. The reasons for the feelings may differ, but they are all the result of your baby's early entry into the world.

Anger and Frustration

While the mother may be angry with herself for what she feels she could have or might have done differently, you probably both share an initial anger at the doctor for not being able to fix the situation or anger at the hospital and nursing staff, who may be subjecting the mother of your baby to extensive and sometimes painful testing. As odd as it may seem, men experience anger at their partners as well. While most recognize that this is not rational—she certainly did not cause or want to be in this situation—all the same, she is extremely self-absorbed during this time. She is more concerned with her needs and the baby than she is with her partner's daily activities. This is temporary, and her primary focus must be on the pregnancy. Open the lines of communication about her concerns and fears, and you may find this healing for you as well.

Denial and Guilt

This is an important step for men to overcome. It is more likely than not that the mother will have more difficulty coming to accept that she has a high-risk pregnancy and that there may be complications than the father. Men are more realists, whereas women tend view things through rosy colored glasses. The sooner you and your partner accept that you have a difficult road ahead of you, the sooner you will begin healing. As the mother of the child may feel guilty for things she perceived may have contributed to her problems, the father of the baby will experience similar guilt in that he was not there to help more and did not take on more responsibility when she got pregnant. As with the mother, these feelings of guilt are not realistic. There are no definitive answers to what makes a pregnancy high risk; there are factors that contribute, but if there was a known cause and prevention measure, your medical provider would be sure to tell you.

Worry and Fear

There is no escaping these emotions. You will find yourself with a host of worries and what ifs. What if my baby is not okay? What if my wife is not okay? What if I leave and she goes into labor? What if she cannot reach me on the cell phone? What if I cannot handle all the added responsibility? Worry and fear are common and expected, and the best that anyone can do is to rationalize the fears and take the appropriate measures to make sure he has done all he can do.

If you are concerned about leaving your wife alone, have a friend or caregiver come over and stay or stop in periodically. If she goes into labor, go to the hospital. Work out your route and have your bags packed. You may also want to have a backup should you not be close enough. In the worst case scenario, you could call an ambulance. The fear of what will happen is an unknown, and as discussed in previous chapters, parenting a preemie is filled with unknowns. Accept what you cannot change.

Helplessness

This is the big one for men. A feeling of helplessness and a loss of control are the most difficult emotions for men to overcome. In addition to that added responsibility, which, as with a job or other familial roles, we know at times can be overwhelming, men in this situation are faced with a complete loss of control. Men are raised to be providers and protectors. They feel that it is their responsibility to protect their families and keep them safe from harm. A preterm birth or high-risk pregnancy takes away the ability to protect. They no longer can influence the outcome, and in this situation, no matter what is done, the situation cannot be fixed. Not only has the man lost control of his family, he has lost control over his own life. His schedule may change because of added responsibilities or scheduling conflicts; he cannot be the way he used to be because of the possibility of the onset of labor.

Depression

Whether this is your first pregnancy or last, the situation is not as you expected. You and your partner had thoughts of how the pregnancy would progress, how the birth experience would be, and you now recognize that those thoughts or dreams will never be. Recognize that just because they are not as you and your spouse envisioned, it does not mean that you will not experience the same joys every parent having a full-term baby will experience. They just may be on a different schedule.

SOME PRACTICAL ADVICE

Men feel very isolated during this time, and unlike women, many times, they lack the emotional support that most women have. Sometimes the lack of having this emotional support system reinforces the behavior to just keep everything bottled up. However, what many men do not recognize is that the lack of emotional release can affect performance in a number of areas, including work performance, physical performance, or performance in maintaining the household financial responsibilities.

1. Do not just "handle it"—Find a way to release these emotions. If they are left unattended, they will fester into something bigger down the road. Resentment is common.
2. Take a break—While you feel that there is no time to rest with the added responsibilities, it is important that you make a point to find time to yourself to reflect on your thoughts and unwind.
3. Never say no—So many people offer to help during times of trouble, but you will find that those who truly will adjust their lives can be counted on one hand. Never say no; take all the help you can get. Not only will this help to take some of the burden off, but it offers a sense of support that you otherwise would not have.

You will find that this will be the most difficult journey of your life but, at the same time, the most rewarding. Parenting a preemie is a process, and just as with so many other things in life, there will be ups and downs. As parents, sharing these feelings and events will only serve to strengthen the bond to your child and to each other.

The following is a very open essay from a father who only now is able to recognize his actions during the pregnancy, birth, and hospitalization of his own child. Learn from his words, and recognize that you are not alone in this process.

A FATHER'S REALIZATION

By Colin Marquis

Though I did not know it, I was trapped in an emotional isolette when my daughter was born. Zoe Kate was supposed to be a springtime baby. Her due date was May 15, a time that symbolizes new life—leaves sprouting, robins singing. The birth of a child is supposed to be a strange but wonderful time. It was all supposed to be so poetic.

Zoe Kate was a wintertime baby. She arrived on February 28, a day when the low temperature was four degrees below zero—no leaves, no robins. The birth of our child was a harried, traumatic experience. Any poetry was lost on me.

Amy's pregnancy was troubled from the beginning. Her morning sickness began early and ended late compared to most, and, by the way, it was more like "all-day sickness." As soon as the nausea waned, the bleeding began. From week 17 she had periodic bleeding episodes, which grew heavier and more frequent. Our fifth trip to the emergency room at 28 weeks was our last. Amy would remain in the hospital until Zoe was born about a week later.

Through the 29-week ordeal I grew more and more numb and consequently more and more detached from Amy. I now know that I was emotionally unavailable, having buried any vulnerability so deep that even I was clueless to its existence. So I did what many men do: I put on a strong, brave face and took care of the daily duties. I made sure the fridge was full, the trash was taken out, and the cats were fed. But the one thing I did not do was make sure Amy was all right. It was not even on my radar screen.

I remember getting a call on that sunny but very cold morning in February. The voice simply said, "Get here. Now." The hospital was 90 minutes away. I made it in a bit over an hour, pushing 100 much of the way. I knew this was the day that Zoe would arrive, albeit 11 weeks earlier than we had hoped. Within minutes of my arrival Amy was wheeled into a birthing room, and scrubs were thrown my way. Zoe was born a bit after 11 o'clock in the morning. I knew this was an important moment in our lives, but there was no joy for me. I watched a silent baby girl immediately whisked out of my sight. I did not know how to feel. The numbness tightened its grip.

Through the fist few days of Zoe's life I never had any serious concerns about her health. I just assumed she would be fine. At the time, I thought it curious and amazing that I could have such a positive outlook despite her rather serious situation. I now believe I was in complete and utter denial. For the next 34 days Zoe lived in an isolette, a physical barrier protecting her from the harsh surrounding atmosphere. Apparently, I had built my own isolette. But mine was of the invisible and emotional variety, and it was protecting a scared little boy who was not quite sure how to deal with these sorts of heavy, terrible things. My emotional immaturity left me unavailable to provide support to those who mattered most: my wife and baby girl.

Zoe came home with us at 34 weeks' gestation. Amy took care of Zoe. I took care of the chores. No one took care of Amy—or me. And so it was for what seemed an eternity. While I was physically present, in many ways I was absent. Zoe lived in her isolette for 34 days. I lived in mine for more than a year.

Zoe is now a happy, smiley three-year-old. Amy and I feel incredibly lucky as her prematurity appears to have had little effect on her daily life. I cannot imagine my world without Zoe. I love her so much. And I think Amy has just about forgiven me for the time that I "went away." I really look forward to Fridays and Sundays, days off for me, when I can just hang out with my two favorite girls.

I have accepted the fact that my daughter's entrée into the world was anything but normal and certainly not poetic. I now know that my emotional isolette was masking real, raw feelings of fear and anger and helplessness. But I maintained a poker face. I did not show my hand because I thought that Amy needed me to be "strong." I believe this was a mistake. Amy and I were robbed of the wonder of childbirth by forces beyond our control. There is nothing I can do about that. But what I now know I can do is listen and talk and support and love.

Chapter 14

When All Else Fails

There will come a time, whether it is during the pregnancy or after the baby has been born, when the feelings of frustration are overwhelming. As discussed in previous chapters, you may find yourself feeling helpless to aid the most important person in your life. The familial instinct will intuitively kick in, and you will find yourself seeking any and all avenues to help your child. As Dr. J. C. Roig discussed earlier, many parents find themselves researching and attempting to gain knowledge without the medical expertise to decipher the meaning of the all the medical terms and studies. It is encouraged that you be informed about your child's condition and what role you and your family can play in assisting your child to overcome obstacles. However, there comes a point and time that there must be acceptance for what is. You child is premature, and as part of that prematurity may come lifelong hurdles that may never be permanently healed. When you have explored all the possibilities for curing your child, you will come to accept what is. For some it is earlier than others, and it is not uncommon for the process to take years. Let me be clear that acceptance does not in any way infer giving up. Children make remarkable strides against all odds with the love and support of their families. It the same type of support that you, as the parent, should be open to during this emotional journey.

SUPPORT

The best medicine for your personal mental health is support. The support of friends, family, health care providers, and others is only asking distance away. Take advantage of the opportunity to share with others your thoughts, your feelings, and your fears. Do not be afraid to talk to others who also have had premature infants. They can be a wealth of knowledge and support. You will find that surprisingly, while medical conditions vary, most of the emotions are the same in the immediate and extended families of those who have had premature infants. As you spend hours and days in the NICU waiting for your child to make the next goal that will bring him one step closer to going home, look around. More than likely, there are other parents doing just the same thing.

Over the years, the policies of hospitals have evolved to the extent that every bit of information about you and your child is confidential. So while your baby may be sharing a room with 10 other premature infants, it is likely that you will never know if any of them have similar conditions to yours. You may never even know their names. While privacy and confidentiality are sacred, we lose the ability to connect to others who are facing similar situations. Do not be afraid to talk to the other parents. They are also dreaming of the day that they can take their babies home. In addition to providing an emotional outlet, other families may have that one piece of information about a test or procedure you were wondering about. Remember that time in the NICU is measured by weeks, not months or years. So every week that passes, someone will be ahead, and someone will be behind you. Ask questions of those ahead of you, and share your information with those behind you.

As prematurity is becoming all too common, you may be able to find a support group in your area through the March of Dimes or other organizations dedicated to the support of families of preemies. The best place to ask is your local NICU. If there is nothing in your area, modern technology provides endless possibilities for you to connect with other preemie parents. Listed in the back of this book are a number of resources for parents of preemies; explore these and others until you find one that suits your needs.

POSITIVE THINKING

When the situation looks so bleak, how can you possibly think positively? As your baby lies in the isolette, helpless and, at times, clinging to life, or maybe just not progressing as you had expected, you tend to worry about what will be, rather than thinking about what can be. Your own thoughts are only intensified when family and friends, in their comforting words, tell you how sorry they are. Recognize that they are sorry for your pain, not that your situation is hopeless. While it is understandable that you are experiencing emotional pain, which can sometimes manifest physical symptoms, it does not mean that you cannot have positive thoughts about what the future holds for you and your child.

The first step to positive thinking is to believe in yourself and your abilities. While you may at some point have felt guilty for the early birth of your child or less than adequate for not being able to do anything to fix the situation, you must now find a way to set aside those emotions. A sense of inferiority will make it more difficult for you to attain your hopes and dreams for your child. In order to think positively and generate a positive motivation, you must realize that self-confidence is what will help you to attain successful positive thinking. This is a time in your life when everything seems to have changed for the worse. All of your hopes and dreams have been shattered by this turn in your pregnancy. What we tend to forget is what we really have. If you find yourself feeling defeated and unable to muster the energy to think positively, try taking a piece of paper and list not all of the things that are against you, but all of the things that are for you. You have a baby who is alive, you have friends and family who love and support you. . . . If you continually think of all that is against you, you will ultimately give those thoughts a power they do not deserve. If you take this list of positive things in your life and you visualize, confirm, and reconfirm them in your mind, you will find that you are able to rise above some of the negative imagery that you have been focusing on.

The power of positive thinking will also provide you with an inner peace of mind. This peace of mind will generate power. Always try to keep your peace of mind by continuing with positive thoughts and using mental pictures of peaceful scenes, if necessary. The most effective means of continuing positive thinking is to immediately cancel out a negative thought as soon as it enters your mind. It may become necessary to repeat positive thoughts out loud. Words can have a profound power—just saying them can be very healing. Another effective and critical measure to maintaining peace of mind is solitude. Make a point every day, if only for fifteen minutes, to sit quietly alone with as little thought as possible, like putting the brakes on in the car. This is more difficult than it sounds because you will more than likely find that thoughts continue to stir in your mind. With practice you will find that a neutral mind is comforting. Since noise is known to reduce effectiveness in a number of areas, including employment productivity, it only makes sense that racing thoughts will interfere with your peace of mind.

Once you are able to establish a pattern of positive thinking, you will find that you have a constant energy. This energy will be invigorating as you have probably experienced fatigue from the pregnancy, birth, and unexpected consequences of having a premature baby. This is important because how we think we feel has a dramatic effect on how we feel physically. You accept what you think. If your mind thinks or says you are tired, then your body responds accordingly. This is critically important since your baby can sense your feelings. Just as in the womb, your baby may be unable to understand words but has a very keen sense when it comes to his mother. The positive thoughts and positive energy will be felt by your child. While there is no known evidence to document the power of positive thoughts with infants, it is a common belief that positive thinking by those with serious illnesses has a useful influence on treatment and prognosis. You must convince your mind of your positive thoughts in order to achieve any real benefit. However, the energy and the influence of positive thinking can do no harm to a difficult situation.

FAITH

Positive thinking and belief in a higher power go hand in hand. Most of us, during our lifetimes, have had some experience with religion, either as children or adults. The choice to continue or maintain a religious relationship is an individual one. However, it is during the most trying of times in our lives that we seek out what may or may not be unorthodox in our lives. There are usually three views of religion. First, there are those who are faithful to their religion. Those who have religion in their lives may feel that prayer and faith are the first priority in the healing processes of our minds, bodies, and souls. Second, there are those who believe in a higher power but do not practice religion regularly. These people find that they turn to the power of prayer in times of need. Then there are those who have not had exposure to religion, possibly by choice. These people do not believe in a higher power but most often are not critical of others who do.

Whatever your situation, there may come a time when you do not believe that you have the personal strength to accomplish some of the difficult situations that arise during the course of this journey. Prayer and so many different religions are open to everyone. If all else fails, you may want to seek out some form of faith. Faith may not even carry a religious connotation. Faith can simply mean that you have accepted that you do not have control over the future.

If your belief system supports the power of prayer, use it daily. Some of religion's strongest critics recognize that miracles do happen. For some, while there is a belief in a higher power, the question becomes, how do I pray? There is no right or wrong way to pray; you are recognizing your own thoughts and feelings and extending them out, looking not only for answers, but for strength and inner peace as well. Praying can help you to create that inner harmony we all strive for in the most difficult times in our lives. Just as with positive thinking, prayer requires you to visualize the belief that the outcome of the situation will be successful. It may not be the way we want, but it will be satisfactory. Without visualization, there cannot be actualization. Talking with God or any higher power is talking with a friend. There is no necessity for stereotyped phrases; use your own language and do it in your own space. Prayer is about inner healing and peace, and no one person can experience it the same.

As the same notion that applies to positive thinking applies to prayer, you must seek happiness. If your mind and words continue to say that things are not going well and that there is nothing positive, then you will surely be unhappy. If you have had a preemie, you have given birth to a life, and that in itself is something to be grateful for. For every negative thing that can be said about the experience of this emotional journey, there is a positive one. You have had the privilege of knowing the health care providers who believe that life is worth fighting for. In their quest to save the babies that enter this world just a bit too early, they have come to touch your life. There are many preemies who are taken as angels very early in life and are never given the opportunity to leave the NICU. Every minute you have with your child, from birth to adulthood, is precious; do not let one of them go by without being grateful for what you have.

Appendix A

Definitions of Common Terms Heard in the NICU

Anemia—A low concentration of red blood cells.

Antibiotics—Drugs that are used to treat infections or kill bacteria.

Apgar score—Evaluation of a newborn baby on one- and five-minute intervals to assess the newborn's needs based on heart rate, breathing, muscle tone, reflexes, and color. The baby's score will be based on a scale of 1 to 10.

Apnea—When a baby stops breathing for a period of 20 seconds or more.

Appropriate for gestational age (AGA)—A chart, developed based on statistics, which states what the norm is for a given gestational age. If a baby falls within this range, then he is considered appropriate for his gestational age.

Arterial blood gas—A sample of blood to test oxygen, carbon dioxide, and acid levels.

Arterial catheter—A thin tube that is placed in the artery of the umbilical cord stump (belly button). This tube is used to collect blood samples and also provides continuous blood pressure monitoring.

Axillary temperature—A way of taking a baby's temperature under the armpit.

Bilirubin—A breakdown of red bloods cells that causes a yellowing of the skin and the whites of the eyes.

Blood pressure—The level of pressure the blood exerts against the blood vessels. The pressure is what causes the blood to flow through the body.

Bonding—An emotional attachment between parent and child formed over time.

Bradycardia—A drop in heart rate below normal. The threshold rate depends on the baby and is usually a heart rate of less than 80 beats per minute.

Bronchopulmonary dysplaisa (BPD)—Injury, inflammation, or scarring to the lungs caused by oxygen, prematurity, infection, and/or ventilators.

Cannula—A small, thin tube with prongs that fits into a baby's nostrils and delivers oxygen.

Cardiorespiratory monitor—A piece of equipment attached to the torso of a baby, used to measure the baby's breathing and heart rate.

Chem strip—A heel prick providing a sample of blood from a baby to measure glucose levels. If a baby is on an IV, this will be a regular part of the baby's treatment.

Clinical psychologist—Mental health professional who has earned a doctorate in psychology. He cannot prescribe medication.

Cognitive therapy—A form of psychotherapy using imagery, self-instruction, and related techniques to change perceptions.

Colostrum—Yellow, sticky fluid that comes from a woman's breast before the milk has let down.

Complete blood count (CBC)—A lab test that tests the blood for infection.

Continuous positive airway pressure (CPAP)—Tubing with prongs that is placed into the nostril of a baby's nose and provides air pressure to keep the baby's lungs expanded.

Corrected age (adjusted age)—Age a baby would have been if he had been born on his projected due date as given by an ob/gyn.

Cranial sonography or ultrasound—(1) The diagnostic tool of choice for screening examination and follow-up of babies with PVH-IVH. Screening is best performed when the babies are aged 3–7 days because most hemorrhages (bleeds) occur before that age. Late screening (that is, when the baby is approximately age 28 days) is useful to find the less common late hemorrhages (bleeds) and for surveillance with regard to PVL. (2) The diagnostic tool of choice for the follow-up of babies with PVH-IVH and posthemorrhagic hydrocephalus. Serial sonography is indicated weekly to follow for progression of hemorrhages (bleeds) and the development of hydrocephalus.

CT scan—Along with MRI, provides a more in-depth look inside. Because the CT scan is able to pick up more information, it is more likely to depict small GMHs. CT and MRI have a higher sensitivity than ultrasound. However, these imaging modalities require that the infant be moved from the nursery and, possibly, sedation.

Cyanosis—A blue to gray coloring in the skin of a baby caused by lack of oxygen.

Depression—Characterized by sadness, irritability, loss of appetite, loss of pleasure, and hopelessness. Interferes with daily living.

Desensitization—Process of reducing sensitivity.

Echocardiogram—A test using ultrasound waves to create a picture of a baby's heart for study.

Endotrachial tube—A plastic tube that is placed in the nose or mouth and goes down to the trachia. They are usually attached to the ventilators and allow the delivery of oxygen, pressure, and breaths. They come in different sizes, depending on the weight of the baby.

Expressed breast milk (EBM)—The breast milk expressed from the mother.

Extubate—Removal of the endotrachial tube.

Fontanel—Soft spot on the top of a baby's head.

Gastroesophageal reflux—A condition that causes nutrients or food in the stomach to come back up into the esophagus and sometimes out of the mouth (spitting up).

Gavage feedings—A small, flexible feeding tube passed through the infant's nose or mouth to the stomach. This tube is used to provide formula or expressed breast milk until the baby is able to feed from a bottle or breast.

General adaptation syndrome—Describes a body's short-term and long-term reaction to stress.

Hallucination—Seeing or hearing something that someone else does not.

Heel stick—Having the heel pricked to obtain a sample of blood for labwork and chem strip.

Hyperalimentation—A nutritional solution of sugar water, protein, vitamins, electrolytes, and calories given intravenously to help a baby gain weight and grow.

Hypothermia—When a baby's temperature is below the normal range.

Intravenous (IV)—A needle inserted into the vein to allow for fluids, including nutrition and medication, to be administered. Common sites for an IV include the head, arm, hands, and feet.

Intraventricular hemorrhage (IVH)—Bleeding on the brain, common in preterm births, especially those before 32 weeks. The IVH is divided into four levels, called grades. The grade, or the amount of blood that is in or around the ventricles, will determine short- or long-term complications.

Intubate—To insert an endotrachial tube.

Jaundice—A yellow color to the skin and whites of the eyes caused by a buildup of bilirubin.

Kangaroo care—Skin-to-skin contact with a baby.

Lactation—Milk that is produced by a woman's breast.

Lanugo—Fine hair that covers a baby's body. The earlier the gestational age, the more likely the baby will have lanugo.

Licensed mental health counselor—A master's-level therapist. LMHCs cannot prescribe medication.

Marriage and family therapist—A master's-level therapist who specializes in matters of marriage and family.

Nasaogastric tube (NG or OG tube)—Tube that goes either from the nose (NG) or mouth (OG) to the stomach for use in gavage feedings.

Necrotizing enterocolitis (NEC)—A gastrointestinal disease of unknown etiology. Parts of the bowel are damaged by lack of blood supply to intestinal tissue. Most common contributing factor is infection.

Obsessive-compulsive disorder (OCD)—Obsessions or thoughts that are intrusive and repetitive.

Oxygen—A gas without color or odor that is required to sustain life.

Panic disorder—Symptoms include intense fear, rapid breathing, sweating, numbness, and tingling.

Parenteral nutrition—Nutrients given through IV.

Periodic breathing—An irregular breathing pattern due to immaturity of the lungs.

Phototherapy—A treatment for jaundice involving placing the baby under special lights.

Posttraumatic stress disorder (PTSD)—Occurs following a life-threatening event; symptoms include flashbacks, difficulty sleeping, and feelings of detachment. Interferes with daily life.

Psychiatrist—A medical doctor who has advanced training in psychiatric diagnosis and psychotherapy and who can prescribe medications.

Psychotherapist—A clinical psychologist, psychiatrist, or professional counselor who provides therapy. Unless the person is a licensed medical doctor, he cannot prescribe medications.

Pulse oximeter—A machine used to measure the amount of oxygen in the blood.

Residual—Using a syringe to check for undigested milk in a baby's stomach prior to gavage feeding.

Respirator—A machine that provides a mechanical means of breathing, causing the lungs to inflate and deflate.

Respiratory distress syndrome (RDS)—Trouble with independent breathing because of immaturity in the development of the lungs.

Respiratory synctial virus (RSV)—A common cold. What appears to be a common cold in most people has serious ramifications for a preemie, including pneumonia or bronchiolitis.

Retinopathy of prematurity (ROP)—A disease caused by blood vessels growing too close to the retina due to prematurity; may cause permanent damage.

Rounds—The designated time each day when the medical team reviews each baby's condition and plan of care. Parents are not allowed in the unit during this time.

Small for gestational age (SGA)—If a baby's weight at birth is below the 10th percentile on a standard growth chart.

Spinal tap—A procedure involving a needle being inserted into the spine to withdraw spinal fluid.

Suction—A procedure that involves removing mucus from the endotrachial tube. The procedure involves attaching the flexible tube to a vacuum, which extracts the mucus.

Surfactant—The substance that is formed in the lungs and maintains the stability of air sacs and keeps them from collapsing.

Swaddling—A way of blanketing a baby, intended to keep the baby's body temperature even and provide a sense of calming.

Tachycardia—An increased heart rate.

Tachypnea—An accelerated breathing rate.

Trach tube—A flexible tubing that is surgically inserted into the trachea to allow for better respiration.

Umbilical artery catheter (UAC)—An arterial line that goes into a baby's umbilical cord and is used for monitoring blood pressure or gathering blood samples.

Vital signs—Measurements of respiration, heart rate, body temperature, and blood pressure.

Appendix B

Medications and Side Effects

It has become more and more common for medical practitioners and those who distribute medications to educate the consumer about the products he is taking and their potential side effects. While your baby is in the NICU, his medications and side effects will be monitored very closely. The following list is of common medications used in the NICU and those that you might go home with.

acylovir—Used to treat or prevent infections caused by certain viruses. Designed to decrease symptoms usually associated with herpes or chicken pox or used in patients with deficient immune systems. *Side effects/warnings*—Rash or skin irritation, nausea, vomiting, blood in urine, yellowing in skin or eyes, diarrhea, trouble breathing.

albuterol inhalation—Used to relieve wheezing. This medication opens the airways and is administered through a nebulizer or metered dosed inhaler. *Side effects/warnings*—Increased heart rate, nervousness, sleeplessness.

aminophylline—Used to prevent spasms in the airways and stimulate breathing. This medicine is usually given intravenously and is commonly used with babies who have apnea. *Side effects/warnings*—Unable to tolerate feeding, increased heart rate, restlessness.

antibotic—Used to treat infections; in certain cases given with food. More common antibiotics are ampicillin, gentamycin, and vancomycin. *Side effects/warnings*—Diarrhea, nausea, vomiting, rash, wheezing or breathing problems, itching.

amphotericin B—Used in the treatment of fungal infections. *Side effects/warnings*—Redness in places treated with radiation, nausea, vomiting, diarrhea, loss of appetite, weight loss, stomach pain, fever, shaking, chills.

Aquaphor—Ointment used to protect the skin of premature infants from germs and water loss. *Side effects/warnings*—There are no significant side effects.

caffeine—A category of drugs used to stimulate the central nervous system. Can help to stimulate the brain's breathing centers. *Side effects/warnings*—Gastrointestinal irritability and reflux, increased heart rate, possible irritability.

diuretics (chlorothiazide)—A category of medicine that helps the kidneys to increase the production of urine. Also helps to remove excess water from the body. Other diuretics include spironolactone and furosemide. *Side effects/warnings*—Avoid excessive exposure to sunlight, loss of potassium, increased skin sensitivity, racing heart, vomiting.

erythropoietin—Used in the treatment of anemia, an artificially produced protein that stimulates the production of red blood cells. *Side effects/warnings*—There are no significant side effects.

heart medication—This category of medication is used to affect the cardiovascular system of a baby. These drugs can be used to treat a variety of heart problems. Some of the more common ones follow:

> **adenosine**—Used when the heart beats too quickly. *Side effects/warnings*—Flushing or irritability.
>
> **digoxin**—Used to treat heart failure by strengthening the contraction of the heart. *Side effects/warnings*—Unable to tolerate feeds, vomiting, diarrhea.
>
> **epinephrine**—Used to treat heart failure by increasing the heart rate. *Side effects/warnings*—Arrhythmias.
>
> **indomethacin**—Used as a blocker to close the PDA. *Side effects/warnings*—Can reduce urine output.
>
> **prostaglandin E (PGE)**—Used to keep the PDA open in those babies that have congenital heart defects. *Side effects/warnings*—Apnea, fever, flushing, bradycardia.

hyaluronidase—An enzyme that allows for things to be absorbed through the body at an increased rate of speed. Keeps IV sites from pooling medications. *Side effects/warnings*—There are no significant side effects.

hydroxy progesterone—Given weekly to mothers who have a history of spontaneous or preterm deliveries. Given by injection into the muscle.

Indocin—In pregnant women is used to stop contractions and usually given orally or rectally. *Side effects/warnings*—Nausea, vomiting.

insulin—A medication that helps a baby's body make use of glucose, which is needed for energy. *Side effects/warnings*—There are no significant side effects.

magnesium sulfate—Used to stop contractions and given through an IV. Requires proper monitoring of magnesium levels in the body. *Side effects/warnings*—Flushed skin, double vision. More severe side effects include difficulty breathing, buildup of fluid in the lungs.

neuromuscular blockers—Medications that can cause temporary paralysis. May be used if necessary to keep a baby still while on a ventilator. *Side effects/warnings*—Increased heart rate; increased saliva produced, which may require suctioning; inability to move; can hide signs of pain.

nutritional supplements—Nutrients that are added to formula or breast milk to increase the calories or other vitamins and minerals as needed. Some of the more common supplements follow:

human milk fortifie (HMF)—extra calcium and phosphorus
medium-chain triglyceride oil (MCT)—extra fat
microlipids—extra fat
polycose—extra carbohydrates
Casec—extra protein
vitamins (poly-vi-fior)—extra vitamins
iron supplements (fer-in-sol)—extra iron

Side effects/warnings—There are no significant side effects.
nystatin—Used to treat thrush or other fungal infections of the mouth and intestine. *Side effects/warnings*—Nausea, vomiting, diarrhea, upset stomach.
pain medication—Usually used to relieve pain from procedures. The most common are fentanyl and morphine. *Side effects/warnings*—Agitation, increased blood pressure, increased heart rate, loss of oxygen saturation.
Procardia—Used to stop contractions. It is given orally. *Side effects/warnings*—Headaches, low blood pressure, dizziness (in the mother); there are no known fetal side effects.
Ranitidine (Zantac)—Used to decrease acid production by the stomach. More commonly referred to as an antacid. It can also be used to treat ulcers or minimize the effects of reflux. *Side effects/warnings*—There are no significant side effects.
sedation—Used to calm a baby. Commonly used in the NICU are Ativan (lorazepam), Versed (midazolam), and chloral hydrate. These medications would usually not be administered at home. *Side effects/warnings*—Slowed breathing, overdosing of medication in the bloodstream.
seizure medication—Used to treat and control seizure activity. The most common is phenobarbital. Others include Ativan, Dilantin, and Cerebyx. *Side effects/warnings*—Sleepiness, respiratory distress.
steroids—Used to rapidly mature the lungs of the baby while in the womb. Betamethazone and dexamethazone are given to the mother by injection into the muscle. Decreases brain bleeds and a common disease of the bowel known as necrotizing enterocolitis.
surfactant therapy—An artificial substance created to simulate the natural substance specialized in the lungs. It is used in the treatment of babies with lung disease or damage. *Side effects/warnings*—Pneumothorax (a result of too much pressure in the lungs), increased risk of pulmonary bleeding.
Synagis—One of the most important drugs for a preemie in the prevention of RSV, similar to the common cold but very serious for babies with immature lungs. *Side effects/warnings*—Respiratory infection, otitis media, rhinitis, rash, pain hernia, pharyngitis.

terbutaline—A drug that can be given by mouth or via an injection into the skin. It is used to stop contractions. *Side effects/warnings*—Increased heart rate for baby and mother, flushed skin, feeling shaky, high blood sugars.

thyroid hormone—Used to treat hypothyroidism. Most commonly used are Synthroid and levothyroxin sodium. *Side effects/warnings*—Irritability, prone to overheating or rapid heart rate.

MEDICATIONS THAT MAY BE PRESCRIBED TO HELP YOU

All of these medications are able to be consumed while nursing.

antipsychotics—Haldol.

antianxiety medications—Xanex or Antivan in low doses.

mood stabilizers—Tegretol and Depakote.

sleep aids—Ambien, Restoril, Deseryl, Pamelor, and Elavil.

This is not meant to be an exhaustive list of all drugs on the market; please consult your physician if you have questions about a drug not specifically listed here.

Appendix C

Resources and Support

PREEMIE BOOKS

Caring for Your Premature Baby: A Complete Resource for Parents
  By Alan H. Klein and Jill Alison Ganon (1998)
Days in Waiting
  By Mary Ann McCann (1999)
Living Miracles: Stories of Hope from Parents of Premature Infants
  By Kimberly Powell and Kim Wilson (2001)
Preemies—The Essential Guide for Parents of Premature Babies
  By Dana Wechsler Linden, Emma Trenti Paroli, and Mia Wechsler
  Doron, MD (2000)
Primary Care of the Preterm Infant
  By Judy C. Bernbaum and Marsha Hoffman (1991)
The Emotional Journey of Parenting Your Premature Baby
  By Deborah L. Davis and Mara Tesler Stein (2004)
The Pain of Premature Parents—A Psychological Guide for Coping
  By Michael T. Hynan (1987)
The Preemie Parents Companion—Essential Guide
  By Susan L. Madden (2000)
The Pregnancy Bed Rest Book
  By Amy Tracy (2001)
The Premature Baby Book
  By William Sears, MD, Robert Sears, MD, James Sears, MD, and Martha
  Sears, RN (2004)

Referral to resource materials does not imply endorsement.

*The Premature Baby Book: A Parent's Guide to Coping and Caring in the
First Years*
By Helen Harrison and Ann Kositsky (1983)
What to Do When Your Baby Is Premature
By Joseph A. Garcia, MD, and Sharon Simmons Hornfischer (2000)
Your Premature Baby: The First Five Years
By Nikki Bradford (2003)
Your Premature Baby and Child
By Amy E. Tracy and Dianne I. Maroney, RN (1999)

PREEMIE WEB SITES

"Cloud 9"—preemiegroup.1.forumer.com
Established by Premature Baby, Premature Child: an excellent resource
for women who are looking for support from other women who have
parented or continue to parent a preemie.
"Preemie Group"—www.preemiegroup.com
Established by Premature Baby, Premature Child: an up-and-coming
Web site for preemie parents support.
Premature Baby, Premature Child home page—www.prematurity.org
An excellent resource for support and information, providing links,
research, and parenting needs.
"A Resource for Preemie Parents and Healthcare Providers"—
premature-infant.com
A source of support and information, written by a NICU nurse, also
mother to a premature infant. Based on the book *Your Premature Baby
and Child.*
March of Dimes home page—www.marchofdimes.com
"Parents of Premature Babies Inc."—www.preemie-L.org
One-to-one support for parents of premature babies. Excellent links to
other Web sites.
"Resources for Parents of Preemies"—www.members.aol.com/MarAim/
preemie.htm

PREEMIE WEB SITES WITH CHAT ROOMS

"Preemie Group"—www.preemiegroup.1.forumer.com
"Parents of Premature Babies Inc."—www.preemie-L.org
"Preemies.org"—www.preemies.org
"PreemieParenting.com"—www.preemieparenting.com
"Med Help International"—www.medhelp.org

HEALTH AND PREEMIE TOPIC WEB SITES

National Perinatal Association home page—www.nationalperinatal.org
American Academy of Pediatrics home page—www.aap.org
"KidsHealth"—www.kidshealth.com
Doctor-approved health care information.

"KeepKidsHealthy.com"—www.keepkidshealthy.com
   A pediatrician's guide to your child's health and safety.
"Med Help International"—www.medhelp.org
   A nonprofit organization providing a consumer research source for
   medical problems.
Mayo Clinic home page—www.mayoclinic.com
   An interactive Web site providing information about medicine, treat-
   ments, and specialists.
"National High Risk Pregnancy Support Network"—www.sidelines.org
   A source of great information and links for other issues related to high-
   risk pregnancy.
"AskDrSears.com"—www.askdrsears.com
   Pediatrician, father of eight, and author of numerous preemie books.
"Preemies Today"—www.preemiestoday.com
   Live support, newsletter, and links to resources.
University of Wisconsin, Department of Pediatrics home page—www.
   pediatrics.wisc.edu
National Center on Birth Defects and Developmental Disabilities home
   page—www.cdc.gov/ncbddd
United Cerebral Palsy home page—www.ucp.org
Emory University, Department of Pediatrics home page—www.pediatrics.
   emory.edu
   Provides a source of information about developmental milestones.
University of Michigan Health System home page—www.med.umich.edu
   Provides a source of information about developmental milestones.
National Network for Childcare home page—www.nncc.org
National Institute on Deafness and Other Communication Disorders
   home page—www.nidcd.nih.gov
International Association of Infant Massage home page—www.iaim.net
"Children's Disabilities Information"—www.childrensdisabilities.info
   Support and resources for children with disabilities.
Matna Health Care home page—www.matna.com
"America's Pregnancy Help Line"—www.thehelpline.org
"Mother Risk"—www.motherrisk.org

PREEMIE CLOTHING AND PRODUCTS

The following links provide a number of different specialty products and
   unique gifts and clothes for premature infants.
"Preemies 'R' Us"—www.preemiesrus.com
"Itty Bitty Bundles"—www.ittybittybundles.com
"The Preemie Store"—www.preemie-clothes.com
"Prematurely Yours"—www.prematurelyyours.com
"Wee Bodies"—www.weebodies.com
"Tiny Boutique"—www.tinyboutique.com
"M3 Preemie Products"—www.m3preemieproducts.com
"Angel Guard"—www.angel-guard.com

"Diaperco"—www.diaperco.com
"My Tiny Hands"—www.mytinyhands.com
Fisher-Price home page—www.fisher-price.com

RETAIL STORES THAT CARRY PREEMIE CLOTHES

Target
Babies "R" Us
The Children's Place
The Gap
Gymboree

PREEMIE MAGAZINES

Your Preemie—www.yourpreemie.com
Parenting—www.parenting.com
Baby Talk—www.babytalk.com
Parent & Child—www.scholastic.com/earlylearner/parentandchild/
Parents—www.parents.com
Twins—www.twinsmagazine.com
Preemie—www.preemiemagazine.com
American Baby—www.americanbaby.com
Plum Magazine—www.plummagazine.com
Baby Steps—www.ivillagepubs.com/newsub.html
Sidelines—www.sidelines.org
Exceptional Parent Magazine—www.eparent.com

BREAST-FEEDING

La Leche League International home page—www.lalecheleague.org
Breastfeeding Your Premature Baby
By Gwen Gotsch (1999)
Breastfeeding Premature Babies
By Marsha Walker (1989)

TWINS AND MULTIPLES

"Twins Help!"—www.twinshelp.com
Products and information for multiple birth families.
Twins Magazine—www.twinsmagazine.com
The Art of Parenting Twins
By Patricia Malmstrom (1999)

Selected Bibliography

American Academy of Pediatrics. *American Academy of Pediatrics: Dedicated to the Health of All Children.* http://www.aap.org/

Ask Dr. Sears.com. *Ask Dr. Sears.com.* http://www.askdrsears.com/

Bernbaum, Judy C. and Marsha Hoffman-Williamson. *Primary Care of the Preterm Infant.* Missouri: Mosby Yearbook, 1991.

Cincinnati Children's Hospital Medical Center. "Medications" *Cincinnati Children's Hospital Medical Center.* http://www.cincinnatichildrens.org/

Davis, Deborah L and Mara Tesler Stein. *The Emotional Journey of Parenting Your Premature Baby.* Golden, CO: Fulcrum Publishing, 2004.

Davis, Martha, Patrick Fanning, and Matthew McKay. *Thoughts and Feelings.* Oakland, CA: New Harbinger Publications, 1997.

Garcia, Joseph A. and Sharon Simmons Hornfischer. *What to Do When Your Baby Is Premature.* New York: Random House, 2000.

Harrison, Helen and Ann Kositsky. *The Premature Baby Book: A Parent's Guide to Coping and Caring in the First Years.* New York: St Martin's, 1983.

Hynan, Michael T. *The Pain of Premature Parents: A Psychological Guide for Coping.* Lanham, MD: University Press of America, 1987.

Klein, Alan H. and Jill Alison Ganon. *Caring for Your Premature Baby: A Complete Resource for Parents.* New York: Harper Perennial, 1998.

Madden, Susan L. *The Preemie Parents Companion: The Essential Guide to Caring for Your Premature Baby in the Hospital, at Home, and Through the First Years* . Boston: Harvard Common Press, 2000.

March of Dimes Birth Defects Foundation. *March of Dimes.* http://www.marchofdimes.com/

Mayo Foundation for Education and Research. *Mayo Clinic.Com.* http://www.mayoclinic.com/

Medical Network "General Adaptation Syndrome." *Your Health A to Z: Your Family Health Site.* http://www.healthatoz.com/

Messina, James J. "Tools for Personal Growth: Overcoming Fears." *Coping.org: Tools for Coping with Life's Stressors.* http://www.coping.org/

Powell, Joyce, and Charles A. Smith. "The First Year" In *Developmental Milestones: A Guide for Parents.* National Network for Childcare. Manhattan, KS: Kansas State University Cooperative Extension Service, 1994. Available online: http://www.nncc.org/Child.Dev/mile1.html

Tracy, Amy E., and Dianne I. Maroney,. *Your Premature Baby and Child: Helpful Answers and Advice for Parents.* New York: Berkley, 1999.

UF & Shands: The University of Florida Health System. *Shands Healthcare.* http://www.shands.org

Wechsler Linden, Dana, Emma Trenti Paroli, and Mia Wechsler Doron. *Preemies: The Essential Guide for Parents of Premature Babies.* New York: Simon & Schuster, 2000.

Index

Abortions, 17

Acceptance, 11, 25–27, 31–32, 128, 143

Adaptation phase, of general adaptation syndrome, 13, 15, 25, 118. *See also* Resistance phase

Adaptive development assessment, 108

Advocacy, 73–82, 98; assertiveness steps, 76–77; and body language, 78–79; concerned or assertive parents, 74–75; criticism, 81; getting accurate information from doctors, 75; hidden or passive parents, 73–74; negotiation, 77–78; second opinions, 82; vocal or aggressive parents, 74

Aggressive parents, 74, 114

Alarm phase, of general adaptation syndrome, 13–14

Alternative worries, 61

Amniotic fluid, 2

Anger, 10–11; displaced, 20, 21; and fathers, 138

Anomie, 26, 28

Anxiety, 4, 21–22, 107–18; bringing the baby home, 111–12; and child development, 107–10; disorders, 58; exercises to eliminate excessive, 116–18; and exhaustion phase (of general adaptation syndrome), 118; generalized anxiety, 112–13; managing, 100–101; Obsessive Compulsive Disorder (OCD), 115; panic, 114–15; posttraumatic stress disorder, 113–14; separation anxiety, 56–57; specific phobias, 115. *See also* Stress

Apnea, 121, 131–32

Assertive parents, 74–77

Assessment, 107–8

Assuming, 105

Automatic negative thoughts, 100–101, 116

Baby blues, 57–58

Bad mother theory, 16

Balancing roles, 47–50

Bargaining, 17–18

Bathing, 67

Bed rest, 2–5, 9, 16; diet during, 3; exercise during, 3; and fathers, 136; physical and mental

consequences of, 31; reasons
for, 2; suggested activities
during, 3
Bedside nurses, 87–88
Belief system, 35, 146–47
Billi-light/phototherapy/
billi-blanket, 39
Biophysical profile, 2
Birth defects, 33
Birth weights, 5. *See also*
Gestational ages
Blame: blaming the caregivers,
29–30, 96; Self-blame, 18–19
Blood pressure, 2
Body fat, 31
Body language, 78–79. *See also*
Nonverbal communication
Bonding, 8, 63–71, 95; bathing, 67;
breast-feeding, 68–70; changing
diapers, 66–67; communication
cues, 68; holding, 64; kangaroo
care (skin-to-skin care), 64–65,
129; making a home in the
NICU, 65–66; overstimulation,
65–66; playing, 67; signs of not
connecting, 70–71; temperature-
taking, 66; touching, 64
Boredom, 4
Bradycardia, 121–22
Brain bleed, 129
Breast-feeding, 6, 68–70; and
bonding, 69; milk expression, 69,
120–21; and sexuality, 70
Breathing exercises, 38, 61
Breathing problems, 31
Bulb syringe, 39

Calm, 37–38
Cardiorespiratory monitor,
39–40
Catastrophizing, 19–22, 59, 113
Catecholamine, 2
Celebrating, 105
Cesarean section, 97, 126, 128

Child development, 107–11;
corrected age formula, 108;
milestones, 109–11
Children, and family stress, 49–50
Cognitive assessment, 107
Cognitive Behavioral Model,
116–18
Colicky babies, 2
Communication, 75–82;
assertiveness, 76–77; body
language, 78–79; criticism, 81;
getting accurate information
from care givers, 75, 90–91;
handshakes, 80–81; negotiation,
77–78; positive interaction signs
with the baby, 68; reading other
people, 79–81; second opinions,
82; stages of, 68; stress cues, 68
Communication skills assessment,
107
Comparing babies, 36, 46
Complaining, 30
Compulsive behavior, 37
Concerned or assertive parents,
74–75
Confidentiality, 36, 144
Contamination, excessive
fear of, 115
Continuous positive airway pressure
(CPAP), 40
Controlled breathing, 38
Cooperative relationships, 85–89
Corrected age formula, 108
CPAP. *See* Continuous positive
airway pressure
Criticism, 81

Decision-making process, 38–39;
difficulties with, 113
Defense mechanisms, 17, 22
Denial, 10, 15; and fathers, 138
Depression, 4, 11; and fathers,
139; guilt developing into, 20;
postpartum, 57–59

Development. *See* Child development
Diaper changing, 66–67
Diet, 12; during bed rest, 3; to relieve anxiety, 117–18
Disabilities, 7, 18, 33, 108
Discharge planner/social worker, 108
Displaced anger, 20, 21
Durkheim, Èmile, 26

Emotions, 4, 88, 93; and communication skills, 91; and fathers, 137–38; managing, 100–101
"Empathy with a Dose of Reality" (Roig), 83–89
Envy: defined, 45, vs. jealousy, 45–46
Estrogen, 27
Ethical issues, 38, 42
Exercise, 12; during bed rest, 3; to relieve anxiety, 117–18
Exhaustion, 100
Exhaustion phase, of general adaptation syndrome, 13, 25, 118
Expectations, 33–43, 84, 92, 93
Extremely low birth weight, 5, 6–7

Faith, 9–10, 17–18, 36–37, 146–47. *See also* Religion; Spirituality
Family, balancing roles, 48–50
Fathers, 135–42; added responsibilities, 136; advice concerning emotions, 139–40; anger and frustration, 138; denial and guilt, 138; depression, 139; expressing emotions, 103; "Father's Realization, A" (Colin Marquis), 140–42; and guilt, 20–21; helplessness, 139; involvement with medical providers, 137; paternity leave, 63; prenatal attachment, 9; sex life during high-risk pregnancy,

136–37; sharing spouse with the baby, 135–36; and stress, 48–49; worry and fear, 138–39
"Father's Realization, A" (Marquis), 140–42
Fears, 4, 16, 28, 89, 96; and fathers, 138–39; identifying real fears, 35–36; irrational, 34–35, 101; and jealousy, 46; listing, 22–23
Federally funded programs, 39, 108
Fetal fibronectin, 17
Fight or flight response, 13
Filtering, 18
Fine motor skills, 107
First trimester, 8, 15
"From the Professional to Patient" (Piper), 97–98
Frustration, 34, 143; and fathers, 138
Full-term babies, 5, 9
Fun, 105

Gavage tube, 69
Gel cushion, 40
General adaptation syndrome, 13–15, 25, 118; adaptation or resistance phase, 13, 15, 25, 118; alarm phase, 13–14; exhaustion phase, 13, 25, 118
Generalized anxiety disorder, 112
Germs, excessive fear of, 115
Gestational ages, 5–8, 33, 35, 87; extremely low birth weight (28–31 weeks), 5, 6–7; low birth weight (36+ weeks), 5, 7–8; micropreemies (less than 28 weeks), 5, 6; normal-birth weight (40 weeks), 5, 83–84; premature infant defined, 83–84; very low birth weight (32–35 weeks), 5, 7. *See also* Birth weights
Giraffe, 40
God, 9–10, 17, 37, 124–26
Grandparents, 50

Gratefulness, 147

Grief: anticipatory, 28–29; and loss of pregnancy, 8–10

Grief patterns, 10–11; acceptance, 11; anger, 10–11; denial, 10; depression, 11; guilt, 11

Grier, Elaine, "Wish upon a Star," 51–52

Gross motor skills, 107

Guided imagery, 101–2. *See also* Visualization

Guilt, 11, 18–21; developing into depression, 20; and fathers, 20–21, 138; and mothers, 21

Hall, Kimberly, "The Little Red Dress of Hope," 126–27

Handshakes, 80–81

Happiness, 147

Health care providers, 43

Health care providers' viewpoints, 83–98; "Empathy with a Dose of Reality" (Juan Carlos Roig, MD, FAAP), 83–89; "From Professional to Patient" (Emily Piper), 97–98; "I Am an NICU Nurse" (Eileen Penque), 92–95; "Words of Wisdom from the Doctor" (Debra Anne Jones, MD, FACOG), 89–92

Heart-respiratory monitor, 39–40

Helplessness, 34, 143; and fathers, 139

Hidden (passive) parents, 73–74

Higher power, 17, 36, 146

Holding, 64. *See also* Bonding

Homecoming, 111–13, 122, 131–32

Home uterine activity monitoring (HUAM), 5

Hope, 34, 89, 90

Hormones, 27

HUAM. *See* Home uterine activity monitoring

Hygiene, 105

Hypervigilance, 113

"I Am an NICU Nurse" (Penque), 92–97

Immediacy, 78

Immune system: baby's, 111, 120; mother's, 13–14, 118

Incubators, 6, 8

Infection, breast-feeding as prevention, 69

Information gathering: from care team, 87; Internet and, 86, 90

Inspiration and hope stories, 119–32; "Little Red Dress, The" (Kimberly Hall), 126–27; "Nathaniel J.'s Journey" (Janet Norris), 123–26; "Time Well Spent with Jillie and Cassie" (Tamala Moore), 127–32; "Zoe's Early Arrival" (Amy Marquis), 119–23

Internet research, 86, 100

Intimacy, 137

Irrational fears, 34–35, 101

Irritability, 4

Isolette, 40

IV pumps, 40

Jargon, 75, 98

Jaundice, 39

Jealousy, 45–52; comparing babies, 46; defined, 45; emotions associated with, 46; and family dynamics, 48–50; and fear, 46; of health care providers' role, 47; of other pregnant women, 50–51; signals of, 46; striking a balance, 47–48; vs. envy, 45–46

Jenson, Amy Hilliard, 92

Jones, Debra Anne, "Words of Wisdom from the Doctor," 89–92

Journal writing, 11, 31, 37, 102–3

Kangaroo care (skin-to-skin care), 64–65, 129

Knight-in-shining-armor theory, 102

Knowledge, 6, 91, 99–100

Lactation consultant, 69
Lanugo, 6
Learning disabilities, 108
Levels 1, 2, and 3 neonatal facilities, 7, 92–97
"Little Red Dress of Hope, The" (Hall), 126–27
Long-term health issues, 7, 107
Low-birth weight, 5, 7–8

Malpractice insurance, 29, 82
Managed care, 86, 88
March of Dimes, 144
Marital stress, 48–49. *See also* Fathers
Marquis, Amy, "Zoe's Early Arrival," 119–23
Marquis, Colin, "A Father's Realization," 140–42
Massage, 65
Maternal fetal medicine specialist, 89–92
Maternal instinct, 1
Medical technology, 6, 7, 22
Medication pumps, 41
Medicolegal conditions, 83, 85
Mehrabian, Albert, 78
Mental health professionals, 59, 116
Micropreemies, 5, 6
Milk expression, 69
Miracles, 37, 87, 93, 146
Miscarriage, 15
Moore, Tamala, "Time Well Spent with Jillie and Cassie," 127–32
Mothers: age of, 92; bad mother theory, 16; and guilt, 21; physical condition of, 13–14 prenatal attachment, 8; and stress, 48–49
Mourning, the loss of pregnancy, 8–9

Naming the baby, 26, 28
Nasal canula, 40
"Nathaniel J.'s Journey" (Norris), 123–26

Necrotizing enterocolitis, 129
Negative thoughts, 19, 35; automatic, 18, 100–101, 116; decreasing, 116–17
Negotiation, 77–78
Neonatal intensive care unit (NICU): environment of, 27–28, 87; getting accustomed to, 30–31; helping in the, 66–67; making a home for the baby in, 65–66, 95; reasons for leaving, 57; support from fellow families, 36
Neonatal intensive care unit (NICU) equipment, 27, 39–42, 84, 93–94; billi-lights/phototherapy/billi-blanket, 39; bulb syringe, 39; cardiorespiratory monitor/heart-respiratory monitor, 39–40; continuous positive airway pressure (CPAP), 40; gel cushion, 40; giraffe, 40; isolette, 40; IV pumps, 40; medication pumps, 41; nasal canula, 40; open crib/open bed, 41; pulse oximeter, 41; radiant warmer, 41; scale, 41–42; temperature probe, 42; thermometer, 42; ventilator, 42
Neonatalogists, 30, 43, 91, 93
Neonatal unit levels, 7
NICU. *See* Neonatal intensive care unit
Nonstress test (NST), 2
Nonverbal communication, 78–79. *See also* Body language
Normal birth weight, 5
Norris, Janet, "Nathaniel J.'s Journey," 123–26
NST. *See* Nonstress test
Nurses: bedside, 87–88; level 3 NICU, 92–97; nurse-practitioners, 87, 93; perinatal, 47, 91

Obsessive Compulsive Disorder (OCD), 115–16

OCD. *See* Obsessive Compulsive
    Disorder
Omnipotence, 17–18
Online research. *See* Internet
    research
On-site housing, 55–56
Open crib/open bed, 41
Organ function, 86
Orgasms: and breast-feeding, 70;
    and complications in high-risk
    pregnancy, 136
Overgeneralizing, 19
Overstimulation, 65–67
Oxytocin, 69

Panic, 114–15
Parental attachment. *See* Bonding
Parents: categories of, 73–75, 94;
    participation in care, 93–94;
    trust in caregivers, 85–89, 91–92;
    view of positive-self-empowered,
    106. *See also* Advocacy;
    Communication
Parents' stories, 119–32; "Little
    Red Dress of Hope, The"
    (Kimberly Hall), 126–27;
    "Nathaniel J.'s Journey" (Janet
    Norris), 123–26; "Time Well
    Spent with Jillie and Cassie"
    (Tamala Moore), 127–32; "Zoe's
    Early Arrival" (Amy Marquis),
    119–23
Passive (hidden) parents, 73–74
Paternity leave benefits, 63
Patience, 37–38
Peace of mind, 145
Penque, Eileen, "I Am an NICU
    Nurse," 92–97
Percentages, 60
Perinatal nurses, 91
Personalization, 18
Phobias, 115
Phototherapy, 39
Physical assessment, 107

Physical symptoms of anxiety, 13–14,
    28, 56, 112–15, 118
Piper, Emily, "From the Professional
    to Patient," 97–98
Play, 67
Polarized thinking, 18–19
Positive thoughts, 21, 35, 61, 116–17;
    power of, 144–46. *See also* Guided
    imagery; Self-empowerment;
    Visualization
Postpartum depression, 57–59;
    diagnosing, 58; factors that
    contribute to, 58; symptoms of,
    58–59
Posttraumatic stress disorder
    (PTSD), 14, 113–14, 128
Power, 6, 78; of positive thinking,
    145–46
Practitioners, types of, 43
Prayer, 146–47
Premature delivery: common causes
    of, 16–17; premature infant
    defined, 83–84
Premature rupture of the
    membranes (PROM), 16
Prenatal attachment: fathers', 9;
    mothers', 8
Preventive medicine, 86
PROM. *See* Premature rupture of
    the membranes
PTSD. *See* Posttraumatic stress
    disorder
Pulse oximeter, 41
Pumping stations, 69

Radiant warmer, 41
Rapport, between care givers and
    parents, 85–88
Reality, and worrying, 59–62
Reality Rules, 34–36, 116
Relaxation, 22, 38, 117; and guided
    imagery, 101–2
Religion, 146. *See also* Faith;
    Spirituality

Resistance phase, of general adaptation syndrome, 13, 25. *See also* Adaptation phase
Responsiveness, 79
Rest, 105
Review boards, 43
Roig, Juan Carlos, "Empathy with a Dose of Reality," 83–89
Roller coaster nature of the NICU, 33, 130–31
Routine, 30, 65, 113

Scale, 41–42
Second opinions, 38, 82, 88, 90
Second trimester, 8, 15
Self-defeating thoughts, 100–101
Self-empowerment, 99–106; guided imagery, 101–2; journal writing, 102–3; knowledge, 91, 99–100; overcoming anxiety, 100–101; restoring self-esteem, 103–5; superseding self-defeating thoughts, 100–101; view of a positive-self-empowered parent, 106; and vulnerability, 99
Self-esteem, 103–5; cultivating, 105; masking, 104
Self-talk, 59–62
Separation anxiety, 56–57
Setbacks, 33, 96, 101
Sex, and high-risk pregnancy, 136–37
Sexuality, and breast-feeding, 70
Seyle, Hans, 13
Shock, 7, 13, 14, 32
Should-must-ought stage, 101
Skin-to-skin care. *See* Kangaroo care
Sleeplessness, 58, 113, 114
Social/emotional skills assessment, 108
Social worker, 108
Solitude, 145
Spirituality, as support, 36–37. *See also* Faith; Religion

Spontaneous preterm labor, 16
Spotting, 119
Statistics, for premature delivery, 16
Stress, 2–4; baby's, 68; and children, 49–50; marital, 48–49; physical reactions to, 13–14, 28, 56, 112–15, 118; and separation anxiety, 56–57. *See also* Anxiety
Stress hormones, 2
Subspecialty care, 83–84
Suck and swallow reflex, 6, 31, 69
Support groups, 144
Support options, 36–37, 64, 143–44; for fathers, 139–40
Survival rates, 6–7, 25, 92, 96

Temperature probe, 42
Temperature-taking, 66
Thermometer, 42
Third trimester, 8, 10, 15
Thought stopping, 37–38
"Time Well Spent with Jillie and Cassie" (Moore), 127–32
Toddler stage, 107
Touching, 64, 122. *See also* Bonding
Training parents, 88, 95
Treatment, continuing, 42–43
Trimesters, 8
Trust, between caregivers and parents, 85–89, 91–92

Ultrasound, 2, 8

Ventilator, 42, 120
Verbal abuse, 95–96
Very low birth weight, 5, 7
Violence, 114
Visualization, 117, 145, 147. *See also* Guided imagery
Vocabulary about self, 117
Vocal or aggressive parents, 74
Vulnerability, 99. *See also* Self-empowerment

Waiting, 33–34

Web site, Èmile Durkheim, 26

"Wish upon a Star" (Grier), 51–52

Wolpe, Joseph, 37

"Words of Wisdom from the Doctor" (Jones), 89–92

Worrying, 59–62; alternative worries, 61; assessing reality of worries, 60; and fathers, 138–39; listing worries, 60

"Zoe's Early Arrival" (Marquis), 119–23

About the Author

LISA MCDERMOTT-PEREZ is a Licensed Psychotherapist and certified Family Therapist, and also the mother of a child born prematurely.